B2 Activat Workbook

CW00521163

Contents

Mary Stephens

1 The fame game

→ For exercises 1–2 see pages 8–9 in your Students' Book.

Vocabulary

1 Choose the correct preposition to complete the sentences.

1 On their recent tour, *Shout* played to audiences of about 5,000 *in/on* average.
2 Producers are excited *about/from* working with their talented new singer.
3 Being a celebrity is different *from/in* what I'd expected.
4 Fans looked at the singer's punk hairstyle *on/in* amazement.
5 Blues singer Lamar has been *on/in* tour again.
6 Are you a fan *from/of* adventure movies?
7 I've never heard *of/in* that actor before.
8 I've lost interest *in/at* that DVD so we can go out now.
9 I love Eminem but Mum says his music sounds tuneless *at/to* her ears.
10 Whatever you do in life, you should be true *to/for* yourself.
11 I've won a place at drama school and I could never wish *for/on* anything better!
12 Victoria Beckham was famous *in/for* singing with the *Spice Girls* long before she met David.

2 Complete the sentences with the correct adjectives.

brilliant cynical ~~dull~~ sincere severe natural unaffected

1 I thought the Shakespeare play would be ....dull.......... and boring but it was great!
2 I'm not lying – I'm completely ....
3 Concert organisers gave fans .... warnings about the dangers of climbing onto the stage.
4 There's no need to worry about how you look on the camera – just relax and be ....!
5 I believed everything the producer promised us, but the other members of our band were much more ....
6 The latest James Bond film was .... and I enjoyed every minute of it!
7 I thought Will Young would change for the worse when he became a celebrity but he's completely .... by his success.

Reading

1 Read the text and choose the best answer, A, B, C or D.

1 What is the meaning of 'head for' in paragraph 1?
  A leave
  B go towards
  C avoid
  D think about
2 Why were *Love Bites* so keen to be successful?
  A They didn't want to worry about exams.
  B It was a great way to meet boys.
  C They wanted to live somewhere more exciting.
  D It was the easiest way to make money.
3 To attract the attention of a recording company, the girls had to …
  A do something clever and original.
  B give concerts in local venues.
  C get in touch with a family friend.
  D publicise the band on a computer website.
4 'The real deal' in paragraph 4 means …
  A genuine.
  B independent.
  C intelligent.
  D ambitious.
5 When it comes to marketing, the members of *Love Bites*
  A think their public image is more important than their music.
  B are unhappy about changing the way they look.
  C want to change their music to reflect their image.
  D believe their image is due to their own actions.
6 'Rows' in paragraph 6 means …
  A discussions.
  B noises.
  C disagreements.
  D concerts.
7 'Those' in paragraph 7 refers to …
  A the radio and TV companies.
  B the interviews.
  C the media bodies.
  D the girls.
8 How does Nicki react to the suggestion that girls can't handle guitars?
  A She's amused by it.
  B She strongly rejects it.
  C She's worried about it.
  D She partly agrees with it.

Love Bites

1 It's an age-old story: four mates with rock 'n' roll dreams live in a sleepy town where the only entertainment is one multiplex cinema. They form a band so that they can escape it all and head for the bright lights of the city.

2 For girl band *Love Bites*, making music was their ticket out of small-town suburbia. And considering how young they were when they got together – their early teens – they worked amazingly hard to achieve their dream. While most teenagers were preoccupied with exam hell and chasing boys, the quartet – whose influences include singers and bands like *T-Rex, Elvis* and *Black Sabbath* – had only one mission in mind: to get a record deal.

3 The friends got the idea for the band during a school trip to Germany. They started out by rehearsing in garages, deafening their neighbours with the volume of their music! Their first gigs took place in dingy village halls, in front of family members. They were desperate for a wider audience, but without any contacts in the record industry, the girls had to rely on their ingenuity. They logged onto the internet, saw an advert for a girl band, and rang up. The record company thought they were too young but asked them to send in a demonstration CD anyway. This was quickly followed up with an interview. 'They thought we had potential, so they offered us a contract,' smiles Nicki.

4 The band's line-up is as follows: Aimee, 16, plays lead guitar; Nicki, 17, is on rhythm guitar; Dani, 16, plays bass; and Hannah, 15, is the drummer. And their music? 'Punk pop with a slice of rock music' is how Nicki describes it. The band are keen to stress that they're the real deal, not a group of girls hyped up by a cynical record company, as often happens these days. 'We write all our own material, and play our own instruments,' Nicki explains. 'We play live

music, too. We aren't a put-together band because we've always been friends. We just got bored with hanging around a park so we formed a band. Aimee's been playing guitar since she was nine. Aimee and Dani actually wrote our first song in the back of a science class.'

5 The band has a strong, marketable look, which they claim is all down to them. Although they want the music to do the talking, the band realise that how they come across is a vital part of the package. 'It's about the music, but you need an image that the kids can relate to,' Nicki explains. 'I like to dress punky; Dani's glamorous. Our clothes suit our different personalities.'

6 The girls talk excitedly about how they've taken over a three-storey house in London, which they share with their tour manager. So are there many rock star rows when they're home together? 'The only arguments we have are about music,' laughs Nicki. 'Aimee and Hannah share the bottom floor and Dani and I share the top.' 'They've got a bigger stereo than us, so we have music wars and turn the music up and down,' says Dani, with a chuckle.

7 *Love Bites* are in the midst of a jam-packed schedule. Currently the girls are promoting their new single, so they've got a round of interviews to do with radio and TV companies and other media bodies. When those are finished, there's their debut album to finish off. And as well as all that, they have a school tour awaiting them.

8 So what would these young rockers say to those ageing, mainly male journalists who, confronted with the sight of a new female band, argue that women just can't handle guitars? 'I think if girls want to start a band, they should,' declares Nicki, defiantly. 'Girls can play guitars – and we'll prove that.'

Entertainment

→ For exercises 1–4 see pages 10 and 14 in your Students' Book.

1 **Complete the sentence with a suitable word. The first letter has been given.**

1 The band asked the .... audience .... to clap their hands.
2 Would you like to be a c....................... on a reality show?
3 My brother's band are going to play a g....................... in front of hundreds of people!
4 Teenagers who go on shows like *Pop Idol* are hoping for instant s....................... .
5 Thousands of people attended the concert, which was held in a huge outdoor s....................... .
6 The singer had a bad cold but he still gave an amazing p....................... .
7 There are some great tracks on *Shout's* latest a....................... .
8 Before we can perform on TV, we have to pass an a....................... .
9 The boyband are going on a world t....................... next year.
10 You've got to have a lot of t....................... to get a part in a Broadway play.

2 **Choose the word that best completes the sentence.**

1 When singer Daniel Bedingfield performed his latest hit, he .A. the house down!
   A brought   **B** took
2 I've got a starring role in a Hollywood film and I still can't get my head ..... the idea!
   A behind   **B** round
3 My favourite song has reached the number one ..... .
   A spot   **B** place
4 I'd like to be a ..... on a quiz show like *Who Wants to Be a Millionaire*.
   A participant   **B** contestant
5 *The Kaiser Chiefs* will be playing ..... tonight.
   A live   **B** life
6 I love all the songs on my *Take That* .....!
   A single   **B** album
7 Members of the fan ..... will receive free tickets for the show.
   A group   **B** club
8 It felt brilliant to stand on ..... in front of such a big audience.
   A stage   **B** backstage
9 Everyone loved the concert and agreed it was a great ..... .
   A flop   **B** success

3 **Complete the sentences with these prepositions.**

along   back   ~~for~~   out   through   up

1 You've got nothing to lose by entering the singing competition, so why not go .... for .... it?
2 If we set .... now, we'll be in time for the concert.
3 Reality show winners sometimes end .... with nothing but broken dreams.
4 Opportunities to appear on prime-time TV don't come .... very often.
5 That contestant's got an amazing voice so I'm sure he'll get .... to the finals.
6 When the actor failed his audition, he had to fight .... the tears.

4 **Complete the sentences with the correct form of the words in capitals.**

1 I need to .... broaden .... my knowledge of classical music.   BROAD
2 I love all forms of ...., including ballet and opera.   ENTERTAIN
3 *Phantom of the Opera* is a .... musical show.   SENSATION

4 During her ...., Kylie Minogue lived in Australia.   YOUNG
5 The mid 20th century saw the .... of pop music.   ARRIVE
6 *The Beatles* achieved huge .... in the 1960s.   POPULAR
7 You need to .... your muscles if you want to enter the Strongest Man competition.   STRONG
8 The money they earn from their tour will .... the band to buy more instruments.   ABLE
9 Thieves sometimes target people at pop concerts so be .... with your wallet!   CARE
10 Listening to old blues albums is my dad's idea of ....!   HAPPY

Present tenses

➜ For exercises 1–4 see pages 11 and 15 in your Students' Book.

1 Choose the word or phrase that best completes the sentence.

1 My fingers are sore because I .C.. the guitar all day.
   A am playing   **B** have played
   C have been playing
2 Sarah ..... on stage a number of times.
   A has acted   **B** is acting
   C has been acting
3 Shayne Ward ..... Europe at the moment.
   A has toured   **B** tours
   C is touring
4 ..... with my CD player yet?
   A Are you finishing   **B** Have you finished
   C Do you finish
5 Listen! They ..... my favourite song!
   A play   **B** are playing
   C have been playing
6 Successful pop stars ..... a lot of money.
   A earn   **B** are earning
   C have earned
7 Laura's hot because ..... .
   A she's run   **B** she runs
   C she's been running
8 Every time I ..... that song, I want to dance!
   A hear   **B** have heard
   C am hearing

Watch out!

Avoid using the negative form of the present perfect continuous.
I haven't played the guitar for ages. NOT
I haven't been playing the guitar for ages.

2 Complete the sentences with the correct form of the verbs in brackets.

1 We can't buy tickets for the gig because we ......**have spent**...... (spend) all our money.
2 Your eyes look very red. .... (you/cry)?
3 What .... (you/think) of *McFly's* latest album?
4 I .... (practise) the guitar for hours and my fingers are all red!
5 .... (you/listen) to the CDs I lent you yet?
6 Oh be quiet! You .... (always/complain) about something!
7 We .... (just/finish) rehearsals for next month's school concert.
8 Wow! Are those new jeans? They .... (look) great!

3 Complete the text with the correct form of the verbs in brackets.

Lee Mead 1) ..**has been singing**.. (sing) professionally for the past five years. He 2) .... (perform) on cruise ships, and 3) .... (be) an understudy in stage musicals. But he 4) .... (never/play) the leading role in a show. All that could change tonight because Lee 5) .... (manage) to get through to the finals of TV reality show *Any Dream Will Do*. The show 6) .... (follow) the usual format: every week a group of contestants 7) .... (perform) on stage in front of a panel of judges. At the end of the evening, viewers 8) .... (vote) to decide which unlucky contestant must leave the competition. The prize everyone 9) .... (fight) for is the chance to play Joseph in the musical show *Joseph and the Amazing Technicolour Dreamcoat* in London's West End. Lee 10) .... (want) the part very much. At present he 11) ....(work) as an understudy so he only 12) .... (go) on stage when another actor 13) .... (get) sick. He 14) .... (work) hard to get where he is but he wants more. He 15) .... (believe) he'd make a perfect Joseph and 16) .... (hope) the public agree. Will his dreams come true? We'll find out tonight!

4 Choose the word or phrase that best completes the sentence.

1 When I was a student, I .A.. in Paris for six months.
   A lived   **B** have lived
2 They ..... two new series of *Dr Who* and there are likely to be more next year.
   A made   **B** have made
3 We can all go home now because we ..... recording the programme.
   A finished   **B** have finished
4 My brother ..... to do television studies at university.
   A decides   **B** has decided
5 Paul McCartney ..... songs for years and he's still in the song-writing business.
   A has sung   **B** has been singing
6 Our neighbour ..... a TV star before she got married.
   A was   **B** has been

Use your English

1 Complete the text with the correct form of the words in brackets.

Boy Bands!

The pop world is full of 'manufactured' bands. They often look 1) ......wonderful...... (wonder), and some of them are brilliant 2) .... (dance), too. But although they look 3) .... (sensation), their records are often boring. Some bands don't even sing or play very 4) .... (good)! If they have to perform 5) .... (life), they panic. They're 6) .... (fame), but they don't have much talent! But, UK pop band McFly are different. They are fantastic 7) .... (sing) and amazing musicians. They're 8) .... (real) good at writing songs, too! Their latest album contains all kinds of 9) .... (interest) music, including theatre music. That's why the band's 10) .... (popular) is growing fast. In fact, McFly are so 11) .... (success) they could become one of the big pop bands of history.

2 Rewrite the sentences using the words in capitals. Use between two and five words, including the word given.

1 He started his singing career last year.
FOR
He .has been singing for. a year.

2 John doesn't take part in school concerts very often.
SELDOM
John .... school concerts.

3 It's ages since Kate phoned me.
NOT
Kate .... ages.

4 We formed the dance group a year ago.
HAVE
We .... together for a year.

5 He's not keen on performing live.
LIKE
He .... performing live.

6 This is our first visit to Africa.
NEVER
We .... Africa before.

7 He hasn't sung in public for a year.
SINCE
It's a year .... in public.

8 Journalists criticise the actress a lot, which she finds depressing.
ALWAYS
Journalists .... the actress.

Writing *a letter of application*

→ For exercises 1–6 see pages 16–17 in your Students' Book.

1 Read the advertisement below. Then choose the correct answers to the questions.

HAVE YOU GOT TALENT?

We're looking for teenagers from all over the world to appear in a TV talent show.

- Can you sing, dance or play a musical instrument? Are you a solo performer or part of a group?
- What experience do you have of entertaining an audience?
- How would you cope with the pressures of the show?

Write to me, the organiser, telling me about yourself/your group and explaining why I should choose you to take part in the show.

1 What must you write?
   a) an essay   **b)** a letter
2 Who is going to read your letter?
   a) a friend   **b)** a stranger
3 What style should you use?
   a) formal   **b)** informal?
4 How can you begin and end your letter?
   a) Dear organiser
       That's all for now.
       Best wishes,
   b) Dear sir/madam
       Look forward to hearing from you.
       Yours faithfully,

2 What information <u>should</u> you include in your letter? Tick the points below.

a   what I am studying at school
b   what I can do (sing, dance, play an instrument, etc.)
c   why I sometimes feel shy in public
d   whether I usually perform alone or with others
e   what I look like/how I like to dress
f   past experience
g   who my favourite bands are
h   why I'd be a good choice for the show
i   why I wouldn't find the show stressful

3 Decide where the points you have ticked should go on the paragraph plan below and add them in.

Dear ... (salutation),
Paragraph 1: my reason for writing = to apply to be in the TV talent show
Paragraph 2: ....
Paragraph 3: ....
... I look forward to ... (closing remarks)
Yours faithfully, (signing off)
.... (your name).......

4 Use these notes to form sentences using the correct present and perfect tenses.

1 I/write/to you about the TV talent show you/organise.
   ....
2 I can sing and dance and I/play/lead guitar as well.
   ....
3 I/study/music and dance for three years now.
   ....
4 This year, I/perform/in public/a number of times.
   ....
5 I/belong/to a dance club/and we/give/shows very often.
   ....

5 Tick the sentences that are formal enough for the letter.

1 I am writing because I would like to take part in your TV talent show.
2 How are you? Okay I hope!
3 I'm passionate about singing and I love entertaining people.
4 Your talent show is a great idea. Well done!
5 If you choose me to be in your show, I will not let you down.
6 You must pick me!
7 I am free to come for an audition any time.

6 Now write your letter in response to the poster in Exercise 1. Write about 120–180 words. Remember to:

- lay out your letter correctly
- include all the information asked for
- organise your letter into paragraphs
- use formal language
- use a range of present and perfect tenses
- watch your spelling and punctuation
- check your story carefully for errors

Do you need more practice?
Go to: CD-ROM, Unit 1.

2 Living Earth

Vocabulary

→ For exercises 1–4 see pages 18–19 in your Students' Book.

1 Complete the sentences with the correct form of these verbs.

dig disturb grab grip lift resemble rush strike ~~struggle~~ survive

1 The spider ......_struggled_...... with the butterfly but couldn't keep it prisoner for long.
2 If global warming continues, some animal species may not ....
3 The zoo doesn't close until 7 p.m. so there's no need to ....!
4 Dad .... me up onto his shoulders so I could see into the bird's nest.
5 Leatherback turtles .... holes in the sand and lay their eggs there.
6 The naughty monkey suddenly .... my sandwich and ran off with it.
7 Stick insects .... bits of wood so you can't see them until they move!
8 Eagles have fantastically long claws so they can .... their prey very tightly.
9 The cat is feeding its kittens so be very quiet and don't .... it!
10 Rangers are afraid the man-eating tiger may .... again.

2 Complete the sentences with the correct form of the words in capitals.

1 Our safari trip to Africa was really ......_thrilling_......... .   THRILL
2 My brother was .... when he found a scorpion under his bed!   TERRIFY
3 I'll have to give the dog a bath – it's really ....!   DIRT
4 Hunting birds is .... behaviour for cats.   NATURE
5 If you cut your finger, it will probably ....   BLOOD
6 We didn't want to set the young fox free but it was the right ....   DECIDE
7 Don't worry about your ....; we're going to visit a farm not a film set!   APPEAR
8 To protect the environment, I'd like to stop everyone flying in planes but that's ...., of course.   POSSIBLE

3 Complete the sentences with these prepositions.

for from in of to up ~~with~~

1 I'd like to work ...._with_.......... animals.
2 I'm terrified .... creepy crawly insects.
3 When I opened the door, the puppy rushed .... to me and started to lick me.
4 The rangers took the snake .... the workmen who were holding it.
5 During the dry weather, most .... the animals disappeared.
6 I held the bird high .... the air before releasing it.
7 We've decided to buy a kitten instead .... a pet rabbit.
8 We were trapped on a rock but luckily someone came .... our rescue.
9 There was a sign in the field that said 'Beware .... the bull!'
10 I suffer .... asthma, and stroking the cat's fur makes it worse.
11 Bees sting – I discovered this .... myself when I accidentally sat on one!
12 I think sea otters are brilliant animals; .... fact, I adore them.

4 Complete the sentences with these phrasal verbs.

calm down ~~find out~~ go back go for turn into

1 When you get caught in a storm, you ...._find out_......... how scary lightning can be.
2 If you kiss a frog, it might .... a prince, or so my little sister thinks!
3 The snake will certainly .... you if you poke it with that stick!
4 That spider looks big but it's completely harmless so please .... and stop screaming!
5 One day, I hope to .... to Africa because I was so happy there.

Reading

1 **Read the text and choose the sentence (A–H) that best fits each gap (1–7). There is one extra sentence which you do not need. Follow the steps below.**

a Read the whole text through once.

b Read sentences A–H and underline all the reference words you can find (e.g. pronouns, time expressions, linking words, etc.)

c Go back to the text and think about the main topic of each paragraph. Are any sentences (A–H) on a similar topic? Are there any matches?

d If so, do any of the words you have underlined match? See if you can find what they refer to.

A Needless to say, the experience was absolutely terrifying.

B When the water reached the tops of my legs, I knelt down and pushed my toes into the warm coral sand.

C One of its front legs slipped over the edge and the great reptile landed heavily on its neck!

D Whatever the answer to these questions might be, I decided this fascinating encounter had been a wonderful start to my day.

E Above them, at the edge of the cliff, the land sloped downhill and there were lots of dry bushes and stones.

F As the dust settled, the monitor picked itself up, blinked its eyes and then relaxed.

G I looked up just as a long, black snake shot out from the cliff edge and hung in mid-air.

H But I had decided that whenever I could save time by swimming, I would do so.

Flying reptiles?

It was the first day of my holiday on the island of Bali, Indonesia, and I had decided to go exploring. I was keen to find out about all the animals and secret places the island had on offer. It was a glorious morning and I decided to climb, walk or swim right around the coastline.

I set off soon after breakfast, equipped with my special shoes and sunhat, and wearing a thick layer of suntan lotion. It was possible to trek around all the island's headlands and beaches on foot. 1) ..... I had my facemask and snorkel ready. And in a pack I carried a bottle of water and a couple of mangos to eat.

I headed along the beach and finally reached a high cliff. Where this tall piece of land met the water, there were several large rocks. 2) .....

I decided I would swim and snorkel right around the headland to the next stretch of beach. With my facemask in my hand, I waded over the white sand, into the sea. 3) ..... Leaning my head back, I gazed into the sky with half-closed eyes, enjoying the moment.

But suddenly I heard a loud noise from up on the cliff. Something was clearly moving very quickly across the parched ground. 4) ..... Amazed, I saw it fall towards me, twisting its body about violently like a broken electricity cable. It had leapt off the cliff so fast that it landed in the sea only centimetres away from me. In an instant, it lifted its head, turned and swam quickly back towards the cliff. Then it disappeared into a deep hole in the rock.

But the drama wasn't finished. The snake – a black cobra – had leapt for its life because a two-metre-long monitor lizard was chasing it! At the last minute, the lizard realised it was at the very edge of the cliff. It dug its claws in the ground to stop itself falling. 5) ..... It was a near thing, but

the reptile just managed to hold on, while stones and dry leaves showered into the sea below.

6) ..... Looking down, it tasted the air with its forked tongue. It looked at me thoughtfully, and then crawled back into the bushes.

I waded out of the water and sat on the beach. 'Do monitor lizards usually hunt black cobras?' I wondered. 'And had the cobra slithered towards the edge of the cliff on purpose or was it just chance?' 7) ..... But as I snorkelled around the coast, a sudden thought made me shiver. Could another reptile appear out of nowhere? And this time, horror of horrors, would it actually land on my back?

Nature

> → For exercises 1–6 see pages 20–24 in your Students' Book.

1 Put the words in the correct group.

frog   scorpion   shark   leopard   parrot   spider
crab   gorilla   turtle   salmon   eagle

Mammal	
Reptile/Amphibian	frog
Arachnid	
Bird	
Fish/Shellfish	

2 Rearrange the letters in brackets to form words that match the definitions. The first letter of each word is provided.

1 ....lightning....... a bright flash of electrical light in the sky during a storm (ngighilnt)
2 d...................... a long period of dry weather when there's not enough water (uhdtorg)
3 h...................... a period of unusually hot weather (etvhawae)
4 g...................... a very strong wind (elag)
5 e...................... a sudden shaking of the Earth's surface that causes a lot of damage (qkraueehta)
6 f...................... a very large amount of water that covers an area that is usually dry (loodf)
7 b...................... a gentle wind (erezeb)
8 e...................... the land, water and air that people, animals and plants live in (mitnnoveren)

3 Replace the underlined words with the correct form of these phrasal verbs.

come about   come across   come back   come up
come from   ~~come off~~

1 The monkey escaped because a bar had <u>become removed</u> from its cage. come off
2 Kangaroos <u>are born in</u> Australia.
3 We plan to <u>return</u> to this campsite next year.
4 Did your chance to film the storm <u>happen</u> by accident?
5 I was sitting watching the baby monkey when it decided to <u>approach</u> and hug me!
6 We were astonished to <u>find by chance</u> a baby seal, lying on the beach.

4 Complete the sentences with these nouns.

animals   ~~change~~   gases   industry   layer   reefs
warming   wave

1 Scientists believe the recent unusual weather is due to climate ....change......... .
2 When you go scuba diving among coral ...., you see fantastic wildlife!
3 At the zoo, we learnt more about endangered .... like gorillas and tigers.
4 When factories release greenhouse .... into the air, they damage the environment.
5 It's really cheap to travel nowadays, which is why the tourist .... is growing so fast.
6 We need the ozone .... to stop harmful radiation reaching us from the sun.
7 After a strong earthquake, a tidal .... may form and flood the land.
8 Most scientists agree that human activity is contributing to global ....

5 Match the nouns (1–8) with the definitions (a–h).

1 pollution
2 conservation
3 environment
4 wildlife
5 threat
6 erosion
7 campaigner
8 nature

a possibility that something bad will happen
b destruction of land by weather or sea
c everything not made or controlled by humans
d damage to air, land, water by chemicals and waste
e animals and plants living in natural conditions
f protection of natural things like forests
g the land, water, air that people and animals live in
h person who fights for a particular social or political result

6 Choose the correct preposition to complete the sentences.

1 They're cutting down the rainforests <u>at</u>/by an alarming rate.
2 The Earth is getting warmer and humans are partly *at/to* blame.
3 Developers are moving in and more land is *at/under* threat.
4 It's better to cycle to school or college than to go *by/in* car.
5 We've got to get serious *in/about* protecting the environment.
6 You can get involved *on/in* conservation projects by joining a local group.

Past narrative tenses

➔ For exercises 1–2 see page 21 in your Students' Book.

Watch out!

We often use the past perfect with *before*, *after* and *when*.
After/When we *had seen* the tigers, we visited more of the zoo.
The dog ran away **before** *I had put its collar on.*
We often use the past perfect in sentences with *by the time*.
The fox had killed several chickens **by the time** *the farmer arrived.*

1 Complete the text with the correct form of the verbs in brackets.

When my uncle 1) ......**became**...... (become) a bus driver, he 2) .... (think) the job would be really boring. But that was before a passenger called Bandit came into his life. It all began about a month ago. It was a Monday, about 8 a.m., and my uncle 3) .... (drive) along the usual route. His bus was crowded and he stopped frequently to let people get on and off. One particular stop was next to a fish and chip shop. He 4) .... (wait) for an elderly passenger to get off when he 5) .... (see) a one-eyed cat jump off, too! He was a bit surprised because he 6) .... (not/notice) the cat get on the bus earlier. Next day my uncle 7) .... (follow) the same route when he 8) .... (spot) the cat again. Only this time it 9) .... (sit) at a different bus stop. My uncle opened the doors of the bus – and the cat 10) .... (run) towards them, 11) .... (jump) on the bus and 12) .... (hide) under a seat. None of the passengers noticed! My uncle was curious but he carried on driving. When the bus 13) .... (arrive) at the fish and chip shop, the cat 14) .... (get off), just like the day before! The same thing happened the next day – and the day after! How long the cat 15) .... (travel) in this way, my uncle didn't know. But it 16) .... (discover) the quickest way to get a fish and chip lunch, that was clear! My uncle named the cat 'Bandit' – a name that was soon to appear in newspapers around the country!

2 Rewrite the sentences using the words in capitals. Use between two and five words, including the word given.

1 We saw a lot of wild animals during our visit to Africa.
WHILE
We saw a lot of wild animals ..**while we were visiting**.. Africa.

2 It was their first flight in a hot-air balloon.
NOT
They .... a hot-air balloon before.

3 I rode my horse every day when I was younger but I don't have time now.
TO
When I was younger I .... my horse every day, but I don't have time now.

4 The streets were slippery because of the overnight snow.
IT
The streets were slippery because .... the night.

5 The party was over when we arrived so we had to go home again.
ALREADY
By the time we arrived, the party .... so we had to go home again.

Articles

➔ For exercise 3 see page 25 in your Students' Book.

3 Complete the text with articles where necessary.

Antarctica is 1) ....**the**........ coldest place on Earth. It is very windy, and there are 2) .... constant blizzards. The Arctic is 3) .... frozen continent, too. So why are these polar regions so cold? There are three main reasons. First, remember that the Earth is round in shape. So while regions in one part of 4) .... world might get lots of sunlight, others will get less. On 5) .... summer day in many countries the sun rises really high in the sky, too. But around the poles, the sun never rises very far above the horizon, even in summer. The second reason concerns hours of daylight. As you know, most of us get some daylight every day throughout 6) .... year, summer or winter. But in polar regions, 7) .... situation is very different. The sun shines at midnight in summer, which is 8) .... marvellous sight, but there is absolutely no daylight at all in winter! Finally, the poles are cold because there is 9) .... ice everywhere! The ice is very white so it acts like 10) .... mirror and reflects the sun's energy back into 11) .... space. If 12) .... ice at the poles ever disappears, our planet will get much, much hotter!

Use your English

1 **Read the text and choose the best answer, A, B, C or D.**

Polar bears are the 1) ..C.. carnivores in the world that live on land. They are found in the Arctic and their preferred 2) ..... is on top of the arctic ice. Here they hunt seals for food, 3) ..... mate. Polar bears are very good swimmers; they paddle with their front 4) ....., and hold their hind legs flat to help them change direction. Sadly, polar bears are becoming seriously 5) ..... for a number of reasons. Oil companies are moving into 6) ..... area, bringing a growing danger of oil pollution. At the same time, the arctic ice is melting due to global 7) .... Polar bears feed on the ice so if it disappears, they will starve. A third danger comes 8) ..... over-hunting. Thankfully, 9) ..... organisations are now working to preserve parts of the Arctic and the 10) ..... that lives there. The Great Arctic Reserve, for example, is now a sanctuary for a variety of 11) ....., such as seals, wild reindeer and foxes.

1	**A** greatest	**B** main	**C** largest	**D** chief
2	**A** place	**B** environs	**C** house	**D** habitat
3	**A** that	**B** and	**C** with	**D** but
4	**A** tails	**B** jaws	**C** paws	**D** feathers
5	**A** scared	**B** risked	**C** alarmed	**D** endangered
6	**A** some	**B** its	**C** an	**D** the
7	**A** heating	**B** warming	**C** changing	**D** airing
8	**A** from	**B** by	**C** to	**D** at
9	**A** saving	**B** preservation	**C** conservation	**D** protection
10	**A** creatures	**B** mammals	**C** animals	**D** wildlife
11	**A** species	**B** kinds	**C** orders	**D** families

2 **Complete the text with one word which best fits each gap.**

Farmer Adam West has been sheep farming 1) ....for.......... 20 years. He 2) .... to think he knew everything about his animals, 3) .... recent events proved him wrong! Spring is one of Adam's busiest times, as this is when lambs are born. He 4) .... standing in a field, counting up the new births, 5) .... he noticed something was wrong. It had 6) .... raining all night and all the mother sheep had taken their lambs into 7) .... nearest barn, to shelter. But two tiny lambs were out in the field, alone. They 8) .... shivering with cold. Their mother was nowhere to be seen. She 9) .... clearly deserted them. 'What 10) .... shame!' Adam thought as he carried the lambs back to the farmhouse. He knew that the lambs needed to be rubbed and stroked all night, to keep their blood flowing, otherwise they would die. But he was so busy. What could he do? 11) .... Adam was standing there, desperately trying to work out a solution, his fiercest guard dog – a rottweiler – raced 12) .... the room. He thought it would attack the lambs, but instead it started licking them all over! It stayed with 13) .... all night and even protected them from the other animals. 'I've never known anything like it!' said Adam. 'I've got three sheep dogs but the rottweiler wouldn't let them get a look in. The lambs must have brought out its maternal instinct!'

Writing *a story*

➜ For exercises 1–5 see pages 26–27 in your Students' Book.

1 **Read the writing task below and answer the questions to get ideas for your story.**

You have been invited to write a short story for a competition. The story must begin with these words:

John didn't usually worry about the weather when he was out walking, but this time it was different.

1 Who was John? Was he young or old? What was he like?
2 Where was John? (At home? Out walking? On a camping holiday? Somewhere else?)
3 Was he alone? If not, who else was there?
4 What worried John about the weather? What did the sky look like?
5 What happened next? What did John do?
6 What was the end of the story?

2 **Look at these ideas for how to write your story. Decide where they should go on the paragraph plan below, and write them in.**

a describe the main events in the order they happened
b paint the background to the story and introduce the main character(s)
c round off the story in an interesting way
d give your story a dramatic opening to get your reader interested (remember that the first sentence of your story has been given to you – what is it?)

Paragraph 1 ....
Paragraph 2 ....
Paragraph 3 ....
Paragraph 4 ....

Check!

Have you organised your story into paragraphs?
Have you started a new paragraph for each new stage of the story?
Have you developed your ideas and used more than one sentence in each paragraph?

3 **Read the first part of a story below. Then complete it with these adverbs.**

anxiously confidently extremely loudly quietly ~~suddenly~~ unfortunately

Our holiday was nearly finished and we were getting ready for bed. 1) .... **Suddenly** ...., we heard Dad call up the stairs. He said he'd decided to take us sailing the next day. My sisters and I cheered 2) .... when we heard the news but my mum looked at him 3) .... She hated the sea and was an 4) .... poor swimmer. But Dad was determined, so Mum just sat 5) .... and didn't say a word. We switched on the radio and listened as the weatherman 6) .... predicted sunshine and blue sky all week. 7) .... for us, he had got it quite wrong!

4 **Use these notes to build up the next part of the story using the correct past tenses and punctuation.**

• the next morning/we/get up/very early
• none of us/go sailing/before/so we not know/what to pack
• while we/put/our things into the car/Mum/hurry to the local shops
• she/come back with/ a large packet of sea-sickness pills, a torch and a new mobile phone
• we/all/giggle/when we/see/her/but we/not/laugh for long!

5 **Now write your answer to the writing task in Exercise 1. Write about 120–180 words. Remember to:**

• start with the sentence you were given
• organise your story into paragraphs
• use interesting adverbs and adjectives to make your story more exciting
• describe events in the order in which they happened
• use a range of past tenses
• watch your spelling and punctuation
• check your story carefully for errors

Do you need more practice?
Go to: CD-ROM, Unit 2.

Time to revise 1 | Units 1–2

Grammar

1 Complete the text with the correct form of the verbs in brackets.

'It's 7 a.m., and I 1) ..... *am standing* ..... (stand) outside a studio in London. Twelve A-list celebrities 2) .... (just/arrive) to rehearse for a reality show. They 3) .... (normally/ work) as actors, models or sportspeople. But some weeks ago they all 4) .... (make) a big decision They 5) .... (choose) to take part in *Strictly Come Dancing*, a reality show which 6) .... (go out) every Saturday. Over the past few weeks, the celebrities 7) .... (practise) their dance moves with professional dance partners. The couples 8) .... (have to) perform a new dance every week. Audiences then decide which couple to vote off. Some celebrities 9) .... (never/be) on a dance floor before! Others 10) .... (clearly/ dance) all their lives. They 11) .... (already/learn) the jive, salsa, tango and lots of other dances. It 12) .... (look like) hard work, but they're clearly having a lot of fun!'

2 Choose the word or phrase that best completes the sentence.

1 He .B.. a polar bear in the wild before.
   A never saw
   B has never seen
   C was never seeing
   D has been never seeing
2 I ..... in Africa for a year when I was a child.
   A had been living
   B have been living
   C was living
   D lived
3 Sarah ..... a new song and it's nearly finished.
   A has been writing
   B wrote
   C has written
   D was writing
4 Why ..... the reality show so suddenly?
   A he left
   B he did leave
   C did he leave
   D he has left
5 The boy and girl in this photo ..... as if they're in love!
   A look
   B have looked
   C are looking
   D looked

6 The cameraman is exhausted because he ..... the bears all day.
   A has filmed
   B filmed
   C was filming
   D has been filming
7 I couldn't go to the concert because I ..... enough money for the ticket.
   A haven't saved
   B hadn't been saving
   C wasn't saving
   D hadn't saved
8 By the morning the streets were white because it ..... all night.
   A snowed
   B was snowing
   C has snowed
   D had been snowing
9 I saw a fox run across the road while I ..... for you!
   A was waiting
   B have been waiting
   C have waited
   D had been waiting
10 Carla ..... enjoy working in the zoo but she's changed her mind now.
   A had used not
   B wasn't used to
   C didn't use to
   D use not to

3 Complete the text with one word which best fits each gap.

Simon King 1).......... *was* .... born in Kenya but moved to the UK 2)........................ 1964. He's 3)........................ working in the field of natural history ever since. He began his career as a child actor, at the age 4)........................ ten. A few years later 5)........................ made his first wildlife film for television. It was 6)........................ great success. So was his next film, about 7)........................ natural history that surrounds the hotels in Spain's Costa del Sol. 8)........................ those early days, Simon has gone on to produce more than 80 natural history films. He's 9)........................ several awards for his camera work, as well 10)........................ for his work as a presenter. But his skills are 11)........................ just limited to film-making. When he's not working, he really 12)........................ composing and arranging music and has also written a book.

Vocabulary

4 **Make true sentences using words from each category.**

1 An eagle		mammal		a shell.
2 A shark		reptile		feathers and claws.
3 A butterfly	is a species of	bird	and has	thick fur.
4 A turtle		fish		fins.
5 A tiger		insect		wings and six legs.

5 **Complete the table.**

	noun	adjective	verb
1	care		
2			terrify
3		living	
4			compete
5	strength		
6		successful	
7			save
8		entertaining	
9	ability		
10			popularise

6 **Complete the sentences with the correct form of the words in capitals.**

1 Performing on stage is my favourite form of
....entertainment.... ENTERTAIN
2 The acrobat did exercises to .... his
muscles. STRONG
3 I'm sure you will .... in everything
you do! SUCCESS
4 When the tiger appeared, the monkeys raced up the
trees for .... SAVE
5 The scholarship .... my brother to go
to drama school. ABLE
6 Performing .... as a pop singer is
really exciting! LIFE
7 Tom is extremely .... and is
determined to beat all the other contestants! COMPETE
8 He went on the reality show because he thought it
would increase his .... POPULAR
9 Sarah feels .... at the thought of
dancing in public! TERRIFY
10 It was really .... of you to lose the
tickets for the pop concert! CARE

7 **Complete the sentences with the correct prepositions.**

about   at   in   of   to

1 I'd never heard ....of.......... Lee Meade
before my friend gave me his CD.
2 Are you excited .... going to the
safari park?
3 I'm not a fan .... talent shows.
4 It was pouring with rain last night so I stayed
.... home and watched TV.
5 Do you think audiences are losing interest
.... reality shows?
6 What are the chances .... you
winning a talent show?
7 I don't like spiders; .... fact, I hate
them!
8 You could .... least listen to what
I'm saying!
9 I never thought .... working with
animals before, but it's a brilliant idea!
10 Whatever you decide, make sure you're true
.... yourself.

8 **Read the text and choose the best answer, A, B, C or D.**

Kate Humble was born in London but was 1) .D.. up next door to a farm. Here she 2) ..... all kinds of animals, which is how her passion for natural history began. After leaving school, Kate 3) ..... on an adventure that would take her around Africa. On the trip, she observed many rare 4) ..... of animals as well as discovering the beauty of 5) ..... landscape. To pay her way, she worked in various jobs connected to the tourist 6) ....., such as driving and cooking for safari companies. After returning to England, she got herself a job 7) ..... tea and typing letters for people in television. She then became a researcher and production assistant, and eventually 8) ..... producing programmes! But staying in a studio isn't Kate's style! In one show, she made a series of 9) ..... broadcasts from the bottom of the sea, while surrounded by giant sharks! Now she makes and presents programmes dealing with all aspects of natural history, including the effects of global 10) ..... .

	A	B	C	D
1	grown	educated	moved	brought
2	ran over	got by	came across	took up
3	set up	set out	set down	set by
4	species	packs	crowds	parties
5	a	any	one	the
6	business	market	industry	interest
7	doing	setting	drinking	making
8	ended up	closed up	drew up	reached up
9	life	live	living	lifelong
10	heating	burning	warming	grilling

15

3 Just the job!

Vocabulary

→ For exercises 1–3 see pages 30–31 in your Students' Book.

1 **Complete the sentences with the correct form of the words in capitals.**

1 During my summer holidays, I have done a
.... *variety* .... of jobs.   VARY
2 I think it would be really .... to be a firefighter.   EXCITE
3 Have I got the right .... to be a TV presenter?   PERSONAL
4 My best friend wants to be a film ....   DIRECT
5 I'm not very good at making ....   DECIDE
6 The chairs in the office aren't very ....   COMFORT
7 You have to get good grades to get into vet school and there's a lot of .... for places.   COMPETE
8 I worked during the holidays and got lots of .... experience.   PRACTICE

2 **Complete the sentences with these adjectives.**

cool   nerve-wracking   sociable   stiff   trying
~~useful~~   varied

1 It is .... *useful* .... to have fluent English if you want to work overseas.
2 Dealing with difficult customers can be very ....
3 As a doctor, my mum has to stay .... in a crisis.
4 There was .... competition for the job but my dad got it!
5 I'd like a job where the work is .... and no day is ever the same.
6 Clare's extremely .... so she's made lots of friends at work.
7 Being interviewed by five people made me very nervous – it was a really .... experience!

3 **Choose the correct preposition to complete the sentences.**

1 I'd like to be involved *on/in* making computer games.
2 As a paramedic, you'll have to think *for/on* your feet.
3 Next year, I'll be knocking *on/onto* the door of all local employers.
4 Do you want to work *at/in* the same field as your dad?
5 What do you like best *around/about* the job?
6 Being a TV presenter is great, according *at/to* Emma.
7 There is no set route *into/onto* acting.
8 I want to mark myself *through/out* from the rest of the crowd.
9 Police officers have to go out *in/at* all kinds of weather.
10 Maria is going to try *on/out* her skills as an entertainer by getting a job on a cruise ship.

Reading

1 **Read the text and choose the best answer, A, B, C or D.**

1 What will they teach you at drama school, that will help you succeed in playing a role?
   A to find out more about all aspects of performing
   B to look for things that will motivate you
   C to discover what motivated the author to write
   D to change the way you speak
2 What is it the meaning of 'break' in paragraph 6?
   A change   **B** promise
   C chance   **D** period
3 Why is it important for an actor to be fit?
   A You may have to do two shows a night.
   B You will have a heavy workload.
   C You may have to help the crew.
   D You may have to act in two theatres.
4 'Downsides' in paragraph 8 means …
   A opportunities.   **B** disadvantages.
   C benefits.   **D** criticism.
5 'Workshops' in paragraph 3 means …
   A training classes.
   B career opportunities.
   C job auditions.
   D acting studios.
6 Why is it a good idea for actors to get work experience?
   A It's a way to learn totally different skills.
   B It's a sure way to get a better job.
   C It's the best method of finding an agent.
   D It helps them become members of the actor's union.
7 What does 'it' refer to in paragraph 2, line 8?
   A acting   **B** talent
   C experience   **D** passion

Life on stage

1 Imagine starring in a hit movie or playing the lead in a hot Broadway stage show. Everywhere you go, admirers crowd around you to get your autograph. TV producers invite you to be a guest on their talk shows. At home in your luxury Hollywood villa, you host parties for the rich and famous. Sound good? Then maybe you should consider an acting career.

2 To succeed in this business, you'll need to have a passion for acting, and to get a thrill out of entertaining people. You'll probably have discovered this through acting in high school or college plays, or from experience of acting with a local group. Talent is a crucial requirement for any actor and it's something you can't learn – you've either got it or you haven't!

3 Some people go straight into acting without any training but most start out by going to drama school. Another option is to go to college where you can take a master's degree in subjects like fine arts or theatre studies. Whichever route you take, you'll need to acquire acting skills, such as singing, dancing, skating or maybe even circus skills. You'll also have to learn about stage speech and movement and you may study subjects such as directing, playwriting and design. If you go to drama school, you'll be expected to take part in regular acting workshops where your drama coach can advise you on all aspects of your performance.

4 At drama school, you'll learn about the importance of researching your acting roles. Successful acting depends on understanding the background of the story, and what motivates the character you are playing to behave in a certain way. You may have to develop a particular accent to make your character sound realistic or even learn a foreign language!

5 When you've finished your training, you'll need to get experience. Many young actors sharpen their skills by entertaining passengers on cruise ships or performing in theme parks. With luck, temporary jobs like these can lead on to larger acting roles. And in any case, such work experience will provide the credits you need to join an actor's union, which is an important step into the profession. You'll probably want to get yourself an agent or manager too, who will help you find jobs, deal with contracts and plan out your career.

'To succeed in this business, you'll need to have a passion for acting'

6 Don't imagine all this will be easy! It takes more than wishful thinking to succeed as an actor. You'll need to be dedicated, ambitious and have firm self-control. Determination and persistence are essential, too! Remember that only a few actors get that crucial lucky break and end up as stars. Other well known, skilled actors may only ever work in supporting roles. Job security is certainly not guaranteed and it's very likely that you'll be out of work or 'resting' as actors call it, from time to time. To make enough money to live on, you'll probably have to supplement your acting work with part-time jobs, maybe in a restaurant or bar.

7 Life won't be easy even after you get a part in a show. As an actor, you'll be working long and irregular hours. You'll be working evenings and weekends and you might also be touring the country, along with the rest of the cast and crew. As well as one show at night, you may have to do another show – a matinee – during the day. Acting is a tiring and stressful activity in itself, so with all these added pressures you'll need to be in good physical condition! Patience is essential, too.

8 If the list of downsides hasn't put you off, and you still want to be an actor, then go for it! If you believe in yourself and your talent, and you're willing to work hard, your dreams might just come true!

Work

→ For exercises 1–6, see page 32 in your Students' Book.

1 Choose the correct word to complete the sentences.

1 Mr Smith gave me a job so he's my *employee/employer*.
2 In the UK most men *resign/retire* when they reach the age of 65.
3 If Mum works hard, her boss is sure to *fire/promote* her.
4 It's harder to find *job/work* if you don't have any qualifications.
5 How much did your brother *earn/win* when he worked in the factory?
6 When you accept a job, you often have to sign a *resume/contract*.

2 Complete the sentences with the correct form of the words in capitals.

1 I'd like to get a job as a TV ......*presenter*...... when I leave school. PRESENT
2 There were five other .... for the job so I was lucky to get it. APPLY
3 You can become an actor without too many academic .... QUALIFY
4 Could you help me complete this .... form? APPLY
5 My sister is hoping for fast .... in her job. PROMOTE
6 One of the company's .... has been dismissed for stealing. EMPLOY
7 My friend's father is worried because he's been .... for months. EMPLOY
8 I've decided to be a car mechanic so I'm starting a .... course next week. TRAIN
9 Medical students often .... in a particular field of medicine, like surgery. SPECIAL
10 I want a job that's exciting and .... VARY

3 Complete the sentences with these prepositions.

at   behind   ~~on~~   out of   under

1 News presenters have to stay calm while they're ....*on*.......... air.
2 Everyone gets fed up with their job .... times.
3 Acting in films may look easy but there's a lot to do .... the scenes.
4 Daniel is .... a lot of pressure at work which is why he's so bad-tempered.
5 If you take a job as a football referee, you'll have to think .... your feet!
6 Actors are often .... work for long periods of time.

4 Choose the verb that best completes the sentence.

1 You can't ..*B*.. a living without finding a job.
   A do   **B** make
2 If the postmen ..... on strike, we won't get any mail.
   A come   **B** go
3 I've got to ..... this form before I go for my interview.
   A fill in   **B** fill up
4 You've usually got to be over 60 years old before you can ..... a pension.
   A receive   **B** earn
5 Some people have ..... a fortune by setting up companies online.
   A done   **B** made
6 If you want to ..... promotion, you'll have to work hard.
   A get   **B** go

5 Complete the sentences with these prepositions.

in   off   on   out   ~~over~~   up

1 Big companies often take ....*over*.......... smaller companies for financial reasons.
2 Farmers often take .... temporary staff in the summer to pick fruit.
3 Our career adviser has told us to fill .... these forms.
4 The company is planning to start .... a new business in our town.
5 Dad's hoping to get .... work early tonight, so he can come to the movie with us.
6 When his contract runs ...., the actor will have to find another job.

6 Complete the sentences with these words.

graduation   grips   prospects   ~~risk~~   security

1 I know you're not certain you'll like the job but why don't you take a ....*risk*.........?
2 Most people want a job that has good promotion ....
3 If you want to study science, you'll have to get to .... with physics!
4 When students finish university, they usually go to a .... ceremony.
5 Actors are often out of work so it's not the right career to choose if you want job ....

The future and future time clauses

→ For exercises 1–4 see pages 33 and 37 in your Students' Book.

1 Choose the word or phrase that best completes the sentence.

1 Here we are at the station! What time ..B..?
  A is your train going to leave
  B does your train leave
2 Dad ..... in the same job this time next year, I expect.
  A will still be working **B** will still work
3 I know you ..... to the party tomorrow, but who with?
  A are going   **B** go
4 By the time I leave school, I ..... three months' work experience.
  A will have   **B** will have had
5 That box looks heavy! Hang on, ... you with it.
  A I'm going to help **B** I'll help
6 We'll be home late tomorrow because a careers adviser ..... to give us a talk.
  A will come   **B** is coming
7 I can't go for an interview next Monday because I ..... an exam then.
  A will be taking **B** am going to take
8 ..... that letter of application before you go to bed?
  A Will you be finishing
  B Will you finished
9 Look at those clouds! ..... rain.
  A It's going to   **B** It will
10 The phone's ringing. ..... answer it?
  A Do I   **B** Shall I
11 Here are your tickets. Your plane ..... at 6 p.m.
  A leaves   **B** is going to leave
12 By the end of this term, I ..... English for four years.
  A will be studying
  B will have been studying

2 Choose the correct word to complete the sentences.

1 As soon as I *leave/will leave* school, I'll look for a job.
2 I'll have to get up very early while I *do/am doing* my work experience training.
3 After I *will have/have had* my interview, I'll be able to relax.
4 We'll wait here until the director *arrives/will arrive*.
5 I'll be able to earn money once I *get/will get* a job.

3 Complete the conversation with the correct form of the verbs in brackets.

A: What 1) **are you going to do** (you/do) when you finish your education next summer?
B: Er, help, I haven't got a clue. I think I 2) .... (look for) a job, but I'm not sure. What about you?
A: Well I know exactly what I 3) .... (do). I 4) .... (take) a year out – a gap year. I haven't decided where I 5) .... (go), though. Maybe I 6) .... (travel) – to Africa for example, and help on some projects there.
B: Wow, that's exciting! So this time next year you 7) .... (live) abroad?
A: That's right. I 8) .... (do) all my exams by then so it 9) .... (be) great to get away from books and studying.
B: Absolutely! Listen, my brother went to Africa last year. 10) .... (I/ask) him to phone you for a chat about it?
A: Yeah, thanks. That'd be great!

4 Complete the sentences with these words.

until   ~~by the time~~   as soon as   while

1 Mum will have left for work ..... **by the time** ..... I get home.
2 I'll just finish writing this letter .... I'm waiting.
3 Please wait at reception .... someone comes to fetch you.
4 We'll phone you .... the manager arrives.

Use your English

1 Complete the text with the correct form of the words in brackets.

DREAM JOBS

Do you prefer being 1) .... active ....
(act) to sitting around all day? Are you
2) .... (complete) crazy
about football, basketball, ice-skating, or some other sport?
If health and 3) .... (fit) are your passion,
and if you have plenty of natural 4) ....
(able), you could become a professional athlete. You'll have
to be a good 5) .... (entertain)! Fans will
pay to watch you, but you'll have to 'perform' for them. If
you're brilliant at your game, you could end up
6) .... (extreme) rich. Some footballers are
millionaires and have almost 7) ....
(limited) opportunities to make money. But if professionals
don't play well, they face disappointment and early
8) .... (retire). Being a 'pro' is a
demanding and stressful job and athletes need all the help
they can get. Most rely on a 9) .... (train),
who can help them improve their skills and give them lots
of 10) .... (encourage). In team sports, the
manager will often give 11) .... (instruct)
about what players must and mustn't do off the field.
Disobey these orders, and you're likely to lose your place in
the team!

2 Rewrite the sentences using the words in capitals. Use between two and five words, including the word given.

1 Over the next year we will start two new businesses.
SET
By this time next year we will have set up. two new businesses.

2 I have to send in an application form and then they'll give me an interview.
UNTIL
They won't give me an interview .... an application form.

3 My intention is to train as a doctor after I leave school.
AM
I .... medical school after I leave school.

4 It's Lisa's fifteenth birthday on Saturday.
WILL
Lisa .... Saturday.

5 You're busy now but have you got any plans for tonight?
ARE
You're busy now but .... tonight?

6 It will take at least a week for them to arrive.
TRAVELLING
They .... for at least a week.

7 I'll discuss it with the manager and then I'll phone you.
AFTER
I'll phone you .... with the manager.

8 At the time of your interview, we'll be lying on the beach!
WHILE
We'll be lying on the beach .... your interview!

3 Complete the text with **one** word which best fits each gap.

Firefighter

By the 1) .... time .... you
finish reading this text, someone,
somewhere, will
2) .... rung the
emergency services for help. Many
callers will 3) ....
depending on the fire service to
rescue them from danger. Could
you be one of the heroes they
4) .... looking for?
As a firefighter, you
5) .... often be first
at an emergency, so you need to
be cool-headed. You are going
6) .... face danger,
so courage is essential, too. Want
to know more? When you apply for
training, you'll be given some tests.
As 7) .... as you've
completed these successfully,
you'll be sent to a school to learn
how to use ladders and other
tools. 8) .... this
training is finished, you'll be
assigned to a fire station but you
won't be allowed out on your own
9) .... the fire chief
is confident you can cope. Life is
10) .... to be very
exciting! By the end of your first
year, you'll probably have
11) .... all the
following activities: rescued people
from burning buildings, treated
people injured in car crashes, put
out hundreds of fires. What are you
waiting for? Apply today!

Writing *an informal letter*

→ For exercises 1–6 see pages 38–39 in your Students' Book.

1 **Read the writing task in the box and answer the questions.**

1 Who is going to read your letter/email?
2 Should your reply be formal or friendly?
3 Which job do you think Steve should choose? Why?
4 How does staying with a family help someone to learn a language, do you think?
5 What's the weather like in summer in your country?
6 What reason/excuse can you give for not meeting up with Steve?

Here is part of a letter you recently received. You've made some notes on it. Write a letter in reply, using all your notes, in about 120–150 words.

say which and why

yes, give reasons

Guess what? I've decided to spend my summer holidays in your country so I can learn the language properly. I'll need to get a temporary job while I'm there. I could pick fruit on a farm, maybe, or work part-time as a cleaner in a local hospital. Which do you think I should choose? Remember, I've got to learn the language, too!

Accommodation's another consideration. Should I stay with a family while I'm there, do you think?

By the way, I'm not sure what your weather's like in summer. Can you let me know?

It'd be great to see you while I'm over! Maybe we can spend a weekend together, if you're free in August?

Write soon!

Love
Steve

give details

apologise and say why not

2 **What must you say in your letter of reply? Complete this list.**

· Say which type of job Steve should choose (fruit-picking or hospital cleaner).
· Give reasons why.
· Say whether ....
· ....
· ....

3 **Tick the items that are suitable for your letter.**

● Dear friend,
● Great to hear from you!
● I'm writing in reply to your letter of last week.
● If I were you, I'd get a job in a hospital. You'll get lots more chance to practise the language that way.
● Turning to the subject of accommodation, it is my firm belief that staying with a family is the best option.
● The weather's usually great in summer so no worries there!
● I'm really sorry but I won't be able to see you in August because I'll be abroad.
● Yours faithfully,

4 **In your letter of reply, which tense should you use for …**

● your personal plans?
● fixed or scheduled events in the future?
● ideas about the future that you're not sure about?

5 **Decide how many paragraphs you need for your letter, and which points to cover in each paragraph. Then complete this plan.**

Paragraph 1 Thank Steve for his letter. Say I'm pleased he's coming.
Paragraph 2 ....
Paragraph 3 ....
Paragraph 4 ....
Paragraph 5 ....
Closing ....

6 **Now write your answer to the writing task in Exercise 1.**

Do you need more practice?
Go to: CD-ROM, Unit 3.

21

4 Tough love

Vocabulary

→ For exercises 1–3 see pages 40–41 in your Students' Book.

1 **Match the verbs (1–10) with the definitions (a–j).**

1	beg	**a**	take something without paying for it
2	bully	**b**	use rude or offensive language
3	cheat	**c**	do something unpleasant to someone because they have done wrong
4	expel		
5	forbid	**d**	ask for something in an anxious or urgent way
6	lie		
7	misbehave	**e**	behave dishonestly in order to win something
8	punish		
9	shoplift	**f**	say something that's not true
10	swear	**g**	threaten to hurt someone weaker than you
		h	behave badly
		i	officially order someone to leave a school
		j	order someone not to do something

2 **Complete the sentences with the correct adjectives.**

homesick   confused   isolated   nasty   disrespectful
rebellious   ~~strict~~   badly behaved

1 I wish my parents weren't so ....**strict**........ . They won't let me have any freedom at all.
2 My grandmother gets really angry if I text people on my phone when I'm having dinner with her. She says it's ....
3 My brother was really pleased when he got a letter from his girlfriend, but when he opened it, he got a .... surprise.
4 I've been away from my home and my family for a month and I'm really ....
5 It's clear that my sister is a .... teenager from the way she dresses and her punk hairstyle.
6 Our house is right out in the country so I sometimes feel a bit ....
7 I understand you are angry but I'm totally .... about the reason. Could you explain?
8 My little brother behaves well at home but when he gets with the other boys in the nursery he's ....

3 **Choose the correct preposition to complete the sentences.**

1 My best friend and I have a lot *in/with* common – we both want to study medicine, and we both love sport!
2 If the teacher hears you were in the park when you should have been in school, you'll get *onto/into* trouble!
3 Teenagers who are completely *past/out of* control may get sent away from home.
4 David's *in/out* for a shock when his parents get hold of him!
5 Clare's been expelled from school and now she just hangs *along/around* the streets all day doing nothing.
6 We listened *in/at* silence while the headmaster told us off.
7 When we were on holiday, we camped out *on/in* the wilds – the nearest house was ten kilometres away!
8 Robert is really rebellious and refuses to take part *on/in* any school activities.

Reading

1 **Read the article. Match the questions (1–16) with the paragraphs (A–F).**

Which paragraph mentions

1	having almost completed a period of schooling	F
2	the failure of a system for dealing with difficult teens	.....
3	enjoying non-academic pursuits	.....
4	a heavy punishment for a small act of disobedience	.....
5	receiving advice about things that may be worrying you	.....
6	doing a temporary job without asking for payment	.....
7	sharing many similarities with other young people	.....
8	enabling young people to do what they want with their lives	.....
9	being treated in the same way as soldiers	.....
10	learning to work with other young people and support them	.....
11	not realising the negative results of certain behaviour	.....
12	refusing to accept regulations if they seem unjust	.....
13	remaining in a place of education for the whole term	.....
14	realising the possibility of future success is in one's own hands	.....
15	regularly threatening to hurt weaker students	.....
16	getting a feeling of satisfaction from doing a challenging activity	.....

TROUBLESOME TEENS

Why do some teenagers refuse to obey authority figures? What kind of help do troubled teenagers really need? Paul Marks investigates.

A
Mark has a lot in common with the teenagers at Red Forest school in Colorado. Like them, he's bright, self-confident, sociable – and knows just where he's going in life. But neither Mark nor any of the other kids at Red Forest were like this at the beginning. When they arrived at the school, these same teenagers were moody, rebellious and had no respect for anyone. They'd made a habit of bullying their schoolmates and disobeying their teachers, and had driven their parents crazy with their bad behaviour. They had no direction in life and didn't understand the bad effect they were having on themselves, their family or friends.

B
Mark was one of the worst. He was so out of control that his parents had seriously considered sending him to a boot camp. Boot camps aim to 'shock' young people into good behaviour by making life really unpleasant! It's a bit like being in the army. You start the day with an early morning wake-up call and are then made to run several kilometres before breakfast! There is military-style discipline. The staff are cold and uncaring, and quick to punish bad behaviour. Anyone caught breaking a rule, however small, has to do hard physical work as punishment.

C
Luckily for Mark, his parents decided against boot camp when they read a report on the subject. This made it clear that boot camps just don't work. In fact, they can make matters worse. Teenagers, it seems, refuse to listen to authority figures they don't respect. It's the same with rules – if teenagers think they're unfair, they won't obey them. Most teens really hate the people guarding them at boot camp and see the rules as something to get around. They become more and more hostile during their stay and often leave boot camp more rebellious than when they arrived!

D
After a great deal of thought, Mark's parents decided to send him to Red Forest, a therapeutic school for troubled teens. It's a boarding school, so students eat and sleep there and only go home for the holidays. Instead of having his own bedroom, Mark shares a small dormitory with a group of other students. Making friends is considered very important at Red Forest and the dormitory system is a good way of doing this. The school is comfortable and well equipped – a 'home from home', as the prospectus says. The staff are caring and supportive and give students lots of positive encouragement to achieve their dreams. The teenagers also have counselling sessions several times a week, as individuals and in groups, where they get help with any emotional issues that are troubling them.

E
While students are expected to work hard at their academic studies during the week, weekends are much more relaxed. It's the time for hobbies and special interests! Off-campus activities include rafting and mountain-biking. Those who prefer to stay in the school grounds can enjoy sports like basketball, football, biking and swimming. Mark loves weekends because he can take part in his favourite activity – rock-climbing! Learning to rock climb has given him a great sense of accomplishment and helped his self-confidence. Climbing with his peers has taught him the importance of cooperation and teamwork, as well.

F
Mark's been at Red Forest for eighteen months now and will reach the end of his course soon. Before he finishes, he'll be taking part in three weeks of voluntary activities – maybe working with homeless people or at an animal shelter. He started out hating his parents for sending him to the school, but he's changed his mind now. 'I'll never be a saint,' he says. 'I have my own opinions and I'm always going to say what I think. But I feel a lot better about myself now. I didn't believe I could achieve anything much. This school has shown me I really can achieve my dreams if I want to. It's up to me to make something of my life. I know that now.'

Family relationships

→ For exercises 1–6 see pages 42 and 46 in your Students' Book.

1 Complete the sentences with the correct words.

arrogant   generous   ~~moody~~   rude
spoiled   stubborn

1 One minute George is happy, the next minute he's depressed. It's hard living with such a ....moody........ person!
2 My sister is really .... She always buys me something with her pocket money.
3 I can't believe how .... John is. He thinks he's better than anybody else.
4 Clare is an only child and she's so ....! Her parents give her everything she asks for.
5 You shouldn't shout at Mum like that or bang the door shut – it's very ....!
6 Once Celia has made up her mind about something, she won't listen to anybody. She's so ....!

2 Complete the sentence with a suitable word. The first letter has been given.

1 My brother has just got engaged to his ......girlfriend.......
2 My oldest sister's had a baby girl so I'm an aunt and she's my n.......................!
3 My uncle and aunt had eight children so I've got lots of c....................... to play with.
4 Karl lost all his family when he was young so a family friend became his g....................... .
5 His mum and dad divorced and both married again, so he's got two new s....................... parents.
6 The old lady next door lost her husband last year so she's a w....................... .
7 She's the mother of my mum's mum – in other words, she's my g....................... grandmother.
8 If my brother has a son, he'll be my .n....................... .

3 Choose the word that best completes the sentence.

1 I don't .B. on very well with my brother.
   A go   **B** get
2 I haven't got time to argue so please don't ..... me about!
   A mess   **B** untidy
3 It's a ..... of time asking John to do anything these days.
   A loss   **B** waste
4 Kate and I are good friends; we've got a lot in ..... .
   A common   **B** similar
5 The students may think they've won but the teacher usually has a ..... up his sleeve!
   A trick   **B** game
6 I could borrow money off my parents but only as a ..... resort.
   A last   **B** long

4 Complete the sentences with the correct form of the words.

~~nag~~   lose   respect   bully   argue

1 My dad is always ....nagging........ me to do more homework.
2 I lock my bedroom door because nobody in my family will .... my privacy!
3 It's not my fault so please don't .... your temper with me!
4 The gang .... the boy and scared the life out of him.
5 It's no good .... with my parents; you will never win!

5 Choose the correct preposition to complete the sentences.

1 I used to like Joe a lot but I've gone *off/out* him since I discovered he'd lied to me.
2 My sister has been going *on/out* with her boyfriend for three months.
3 He promised to marry her but he let her *off/down*.
4 My dad and I get *on/through* really well.
5 The friends fell *out/over* because they couldn't agree which disco to go to!
6 My twin brothers have fallen *in/on* love with the same girl.
7 It's horrible when you argue with a friend but it's great when you make it *up/over*.
8 My brother's been really unhappy since he broke *off/up* with his girlfriend.

6 Complete the sentences with the correct form of *do* or *make*.

1 Cilla's upstairs – she's just ....doing........ her hair.
2 Don't go out in those awful shorts – people will .... fun of you!
3 I hate .... housework!
4 Don't be stupid! That spider won't .... you any harm.
5 I don't want to go to the party so I'll .... an excuse and stay at home.
6 I .... lots of new friends on holiday last year.
7 If you .... your homework tonight, you'll be free to go out tomorrow.
8 Sandra says she'll never .... the same mistake again.

Modal verbs

→ For exercises 1–3 see pages 43 and 47 in your Students' Book.

1 **Choose the correct words to complete the sentences.**

1 If a police officer orders you to do something, you *should/must*, there's no choice about it.
2 I saw Ben sitting in the garden when he *should have cut/should have been cutting* the lawn.
3 Dad says it's okay to stay out late tonight and we *don't have to/mustn't* be home until 11p.m.
4 I passed all my exams so I *didn't have to repeat/mustn't have repeated* the course.
5 It's not compulsory to wear a helmet when you're on a bicycle but most doctors think you *should/have got to*.
6 You *can't/needn't* come shopping with us if you don't want to.
7 I don't think you *ought to/must* speak to your parents like that.
8 How long did you *must/have to* wait outside the cinema?

2 **Complete the sentences with the correct form of the modal verbs in Exercise 1 and any other necessary verbs.**

1 I'm sorry I .... *can't* .... come to the disco with you tonight. I .... to do my homework.
2 .... you remember where I put the keys? I've looked, but I .... find them anywhere!
3 Yesterday, I .... wait half an hour before I .... use the computer in the internet café.
4 It was wrong of you to tell a lie. You really .... have told the truth.
5 We .... a taxi from the airport because my friend's father gave us a lift.
6 You .... drink a lot of alcohol and then drive a car. It's illegal!
7 I .... swim until last year, when my uncle taught me.
8 We .... all that washing up after all – there's a dishwasher in the next room!

3 **Rewrite the sentences using the words in capitals. Use between two and five words, including the word given.**

1 It wasn't necessary to apologise to Matthew, but I did.
APOLOGISED
I *needn't have apologised* to Matthew, but I did.
2 Was it necessary for you to get your parents' permission to go to the party?
NEED
Did .... your parents' permission to go to the party?
3 It's important that you keep this a secret.
GOT
You .... this a secret.
4 He wasn't obliged to pay for his ticket, so he didn't.
HAVE
He .... for his ticket.
5 It wasn't necessary for you to worry about me because I was fine!
WORRIED
You .... about me because I was fine!
6 If you break that window, you'll get into trouble!
NOT
You .... that window or you'll get into trouble!

7 It was wrong of you to do that!
SHOULD
You .... that!
8 It's possible that Jack had a fight with his girlfriend.
MIGHT
Jack .... a fight with his girlfriend.

Use your English

1 Complete the text with <u>one</u> word which best fits each gap.

Problems

Dear Agony Aunt,

I have got a problem and I'm hoping you 1) .... help me. My parents don't understand me! I'm 16, and so are all my friends. When we go out, my friends don't 2) .... to be home early, but I do! My parents say I 3) .... be home by 9 p.m. It's not fair! And that's not all. I met my friends last night and we went to a disco. My parents were furious. They said I should have 4) .... them where I was going. I 5) .... not believe it! My friends don't have 6) .... say where they're going, and my parents should 7) .... expect me to, either. When I complained, my dad lost his temper. He said I 8) .... to have been at home studying, anyway. Honestly! I 9) .... to walk away before I screamed! I went upstairs and closed my door so I 10) .... not have to listen to him any more. If I was 18, I would be 11) .... to leave home, but 16 is too young. I can't stand this any longer! What can I do?

Yours, Emma

2 Read the text and choose the best answer, A, B, C or D.

Family blues

Do you have a good 1) ..C.. with your brothers and sisters or do they drive you crazy? Most brothers and sisters 2) ..... from time to time. There's nothing 3) ..... with that – it's a basic animal instinct. Baby kittens fight for the mother cat's attention. And human brothers and sisters 4) ..... out for very similar reasons. They think they 5) ..... have more attention, or more space, or more privacy. 6) ..... although a little jealousy is natural in families, constant fighting can make life a misery. You don't 7) ..... to be best buddies with your brother or sister but you should show them respect. Getting aggressive and 8) ..... your temper isn't the best way to win an argument. In fact, it's a complete 9) ..... of time. So next time your brother or sister annoys you or starts to 10) ..... you about, take a deep breath, stay calm, and make it clear you want to stop the fights. They probably don't enjoy arguing all the time, either. If you sit down and discuss things, you may find you have a lot more 11) ..... common than you knew!

1	**A** relations	**B** friendship	**C** relationship	**D** relative
2	**A** dispute	**B** discuss	**C** disturb	**D** disagree
3	**A** wrong	**B** bad	**C** false	**D** incorrect
4	**A** drop	**B** stand	**C** fall	**D** break
5	**A** need	**B** ought	**C** would	**D** should
6	**A** And	**B** So	**C** Also	**D** But
7	**A** must	**B** need	**C** want	**D** require
8	**A** losing	**B** showing	**C** making	**D** throwing
9	**A** mistake	**B** waste	**C** miss	**D** loss
10	**A** bully	**B** mess	**C** nag	**D** spoil
11	**A** on	**B** at	**C** in	**D** for

Writing *an informal letter*

➜ For exercises 1–6 see pages 48–49 in your Students' Book.

1 Read this letter to the advice column of a teenage magazine. Then answer the questions.

Ask Aunt Megan

Dear Aunt Megan,

I'm crazy about a girl who lives in my street. The problem is, I haven't got the courage to ask her out so she's got no idea how I feel. And I'm scared she wouldn't be interested even if I told her.

I know it's stupid but I just can't stop imagining how much better life would be if I had her in my life. It's not just a crush like when you collect photos and autographs of your favourite singer or actress. That's just fantasy. This is real life.

I can't talk to my friends about it. It's embarrassing and I know they'd laugh at me. And I can't tell my family! I can't stop thinking about her so my schoolwork is going badly. I don't want to go out anymore either. I just sit at home and worry about what to do. Can you help me?

Yours, Peter 15

1 Who does Peter fancy?
2 Has he done anything about it? Why not?
3 Do you think Peter should tell the girl how he feels?
4 What other advice would you give Peter?

2 Read the reply to Peter's letter. Does it contain any of the advice you thought of?

Dear Peter,

I'm sorry to hear you're going through such a tough time. But don't worry – things are never as bad as they seem. As I see it, you've got two choices.

First, you could decide to say nothing. That's probably not a good idea because you'll never get to date the girl. What's more, you'll spend ages wondering if you've done the right thing, and you'll be heartbroken when she dates another boy.

Second, you could tell the girl how you feel. I think this is a much better solution as at least you'll know the truth. You shouldn't feel embarrassed. Most girls are delighted to find they're attractive to boys, whatever the situation!

Just remember! Lots of people fancy someone who doesn't fancy them. That's life! It doesn't mean there's anything wrong with you. If this girl's not interested, go back to enjoying the things you did before she came along. It might take a while, but you'll forget all about her in the end.

Yours, Aunt Megan

3 Note down phrases or sentences in the reply that contain the following:

1 suggestions or advice
2 explanations for certain suggestions/advice
3 expressions of sympathy/reassurance

4 Which one of these phrases should you probably not use when giving advice?

You should …
You could …
Why not … ?
You must …
If I were you, I would …

5 Answer these questions about the advice letter in Exercise 2.

1 How many paragraphs are there? What is the topic of each?
2 A well written paragraph often includes one topic sentence which summarises the topic of that paragraph. Underline the topic sentence in paragraph 2 and in paragraph 3.
3 Does the letter have a clear introduction and conclusion?

6 Now read this student's problem and write a letter of reply. Write about 150–175 words.

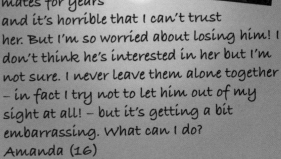

Dear …
I'm so mixed up! I think my best friend, Kim, is trying to steal my boyfriend. She pretends she isn't. But she gets a dreamy look in her eyes whenever he comes in a room. We've been mates for years and it's horrible that I can't trust her. But I'm so worried about losing him! I don't think he's interested in her but I'm not sure. I never leave them alone together – in fact I try not to let him out of my sight at all! – but it's getting a bit embarrassing. What can I do?
Amanda (16)

Do you need more practice?
Go to: CD-ROM, Unit 4.

Grammar

1 Complete the sentences with the correct form of the verbs in brackets.

1 This time tomorrow I ......'ll be lying....... (lie) on the beach.

2 Once we .... (get) to the station, I .... (ring) my parents. Can I borrow your mobile phone?

3 I .... (see) the doctor at 2 p.m. I've got an appointment.

4 I hope Mum .... (make) dinner and put it on the table by the time we get home!

5 Quick, do something! The dog .... (be) sick!

6 I .... (go) shopping. Can I get you anything?

7 What time .... (your flight/leave)? Have we got time for a coffee?

8 We .... (go) to play tennis but it started to rain so we changed our minds.

9 I can look for a part-time job after I .... (leave) school.

10 I .... (not/forget) what you've done, I promise!

2 Rewrite the sentences using the words in capitals. Use between two and five words, including the word given.

1 It wasn't necessary for Mark to go to school so he went to the park instead.
HAVE
Mark ..didn't have to go... to school so he went to the park instead.

2 It was possible for John to ask for promotion, but he didn't.
COULD
John .... promotion, but he didn't.

3 We aren't doing enough to make new students feel at home, and that's wrong.
BE
We .... more to make new students feel at home.

4 It was wrong of her to use her mother's credit card without permission.
OUGHT
She .... her mother's credit card without permission.

5 It isn't necessary for him to work on Saturdays.
NEED
He .... on Saturdays.

3 Choose the word or phrase that best completes the sentence.

1 We really .B. to tell our parents where we are. Otherwise they'll get worried about us.
   A should   B ought
   C must   D had

2 By the time this postcard ..... to you, we'll probably have finished our holiday.
   A will get   B is going to get
   C is getting   D gets

3 She ..... you but she didn't have time.
   A would call   B was going to call
   C was calling   D would be calling

4 I can't go out until I ..... my homework.
   A have finished   B will finish
   C am finishing   D will have finished

5 Entrance to the art gallery was free so we ..... anything to get in.
   A didn't need to pay   B needn't have paid
   C mustn't have paid   D couldn't have paid

6 Do you think you ..... all the songs for the school concert by next week?
   A will be learning   B learn
   C will have learnt   D will learn

4 Complete the text with one word which best fits each gap.

Teens at work

Not sure what job you'd like to do when you 1)..........are.......... older? Well, you don't need 2)........................ decide just yet! Call *Teens At Work* and we 3)........................ do everything we can to help you choose your perfect career. To join our vocational scheme you 4)........................ be at least fourteen years of age – we don't make any exceptions. We'll start by having 5)........................ chat with you so you 6)........................ tell us what you like, and 7)........................ you want to do. As soon as we 8)........................ done that, we'll get you a placement so you can try out the job of your choice. There's a wide range of choice including hospitality and catering, hairdressing and engineering. The good news is, you'll 9)........................ earning a salary – not much, but 10)........................ to pay your bus fares and for your lunches. You'll probably spend two 11)........................ three weeks in your placement. It's not long but by the 12)........................ you've finished, you'll have learnt a lot about the job – and you'll have had lots of fun, too!

Vocabulary

5 **Complete the sentences with the correct form of the words in capitals.**

1 My sister's going to art college; she's really
......._creative_.......!   CREATE

2 You have to be at the right level of
.... before you can take up rock-climbing.   FIT

3 Jason is .... at science subjects but he's much better at languages.   HOPE

4 When I leave school, I want to .... in journalism.   SPECIAL

5 If you keep buying chocolate and ....
drinks, you'll get fat!   FIZZ

6 The jewels are locked away in a safe because they're
absolutely ....   PRICE

7 I'm not .... clear about which career
I want to follow.   COMPLETE

8 You'll never make a good footballer unless you follow
....   INSTRUCT

6 **Choose the correct words to complete the sentences.**

1 When people _resign/retire_, they give up work and live on their old-age pension.

2 She doesn't _go on/get on_ very well with her sister.

3 I'll have to get a _work/job_ to pay for my guitar lessons.

4 He once worked _as/like_ a DJ.

5 I'm lucky because I've always found it easy to _do/make_ friends.

6 His _employer/employee_ was late for work every day so he fired him.

7 He's so _stubborn/arrogant_, he thinks nobody in the world is better than him!

8 She _makes/does_ a living by cleaning other people's flats.

9 At school, they arrange for us to do a few weeks' work _training/experience_, to help us decide on a career.

10 It's no good _losing/missing_ your temper with me!

7 **Choose the word or phrase that best completes the sentence.**

1 My sister and her fiancé have .B. and she's given him back her ring.
   A broken down
   B broken up
   C broken in
   D broken through

2 Please would you help me ..... in this form?
   A fill
   B write
   C sign
   D make

3 My mum's going to try and ..... work early tonight so she can come to the parent-teacher meeting.
   A get over
   B get off
   C get by
   D get from

4 The local supermarket is ..... temporary staff during the summer so I might work there.
   A putting on
   B setting on
   C taking on
   D getting on

5 I think John is ..... Clare; he never answers the phone when she rings!
   A going on
   B going out
   C going for
   D going off

6 My dad's thinking of ..... a new business.
   A getting up
   B starting up
   C making up
   D putting up

7 My visa ..... next month.
   A runs up
   B runs over
   C runs out
   D runs off

8 He would never have broken the law if the gang hadn't ..... him into it.
   A put
   B talked
   C thrown
   D set

5 Use your head!

Vocabulary

> → For exercises 1–4 see pages 52–53 in your Students' Book.

1 Match a word or phrase (1–8) with a word (a–h) to make common collocations.

1	a personal	a	division
2	secretarial	b	experiment
3	a play	c	ground
4	low	d	results
5	exam	e	tables
6	long	f	computer
7	multiplication	g	grades
8	a practical	h	skills

2 Complete the collocations with these verbs.

write   break   play   ~~learn~~

1 I don't want to go to university or college; I'd rather .... **learn** .... *a trade* like plumbing.
2 When she was at school, my grandmother had to .... *lines* as a punishment; she had to write 'I must try harder' 500 times!
3 If you .... *the rules*, you'll get expelled from school.
4 Dad saw one of my classmates sitting in a bar yesterday morning instead of going to school; he told her not to .... *truant* again or he'd report her.

3 Choose the correct preposition to complete the sentences.

1 I think I'm going to do well *on/in* my exams.
2 Most of us rely *in/on* calculators to do our sums for us.
3 Which period of history are you planning to focus *on/in* now?
4 At university I'll be able to study my favourite subject *on/in* depth.
5 My sister's not a very good student – she's always *in/on* trouble!

4 Complete the sentences with the correct form of these verbs.

involve   ~~muck about~~   predict   rely

1 If you ..... **muck about** ..... and disturb the class, you'll get into trouble with the teacher.
2 Can I .... on you to wake me up in time tomorrow?
3 My teacher .... I'll pass all my exams – I hope she's right!
4 I'm impressed you want to study law, but do you realise how much work it ....?

Reading

1 Read the text and choose the best answer, A, B, C or D.

1 What was the main aim of the teachers taking part in *The Unteachables*?
   A To star in a reality TV show.   B To keep the viewers amused.
   C To win a competition.   D To succeed in a difficult task.
2 What does 'go to pieces' in paragraph 2 mean?
   A show off   B start laughing
   C get nervous   D play about
3 Why did Beadle make punctuation into a kung fu activity?
   A Because he didn't take the subject seriously.
   B Because his pupils didn't enjoy book learning.
   C Because he was secretly worried about their weaknesses.
   D Because it made his pupils look stronger.
4 In paragraph 4, how does the author say some viewers might respond to Beadle's teaching style?
   A They might disapprove.   B They might be amazed.
   C They might be pleased.   D They might be puzzled.
5 According to the author, what does Grace's T-shirt tell us about her character?
   A She's artistic.   B She's rebellious.
   C She's selfish.   D She's stylish.
6 In paragraph 6 Beadle implies that good teachers
   A don't need to be experts.
   B use a variety of teaching techniques.
   C should never use textbooks.
   D mustn't be old or boring.
7 In paragraph 7, the author implies that Beadle's teaching methods
   A are ineffective.   B are ridiculous.
   C are successful.   D are a waste of time.
8 What does 'disrupt' mean in the final paragraph?
   A improve   B widen
   C influence   D spoil

Are they unteachables?

1 Can you imagine reading Shakespeare to a herd of cows? Sound weird? Well, that's what sixteen students had to do in a TV series called *The Unteachables*. But this wasn't just reality TV; it was a genuine experiment. The teachers on the series had been set a challenge: could they turn about a class of the most badly behaved schoolkids in the country in just five months, and make them into decent students?

2 One of the teachers challenged to interest these 'nightmare' teenagers in learning was Phil Beadle. Phil is a genius. Reading to the cows was just one of his techniques for making learning fun. It had a serious purpose, of course. A boy in his class would go to pieces if asked to read in front of his schoolmates. How did Beadle persuade him to conquer his fears without making him feel stupid? By making it a laugh, of course!

3 Beadle played to his pupils' strengths, instead of worrying them about their weaknesses. And because they weren't naturally academic, he got them moving around. In one programme, viewers saw him in a field, dressed in a smart suit, playing punctuation kung fu with his class. He shouted 'Question mark!' and then joined in as the kids did the relevant kung fu move, bouncing about and shouting in unison. It was grammar teaching like you've never known it before!

4 Beadle used to be a rock musician but gave up music because he wanted to teach English. And he's passionate about the job. Winning the 'Schoolteacher of the Year' award got him noticed and made him an ideal choice for *The Unteachables*. Viewers may shake their heads at some of his methods. When he first met his TV pupils, for example, he used rather bad language. But Beadle shrugs off criticism. 'You need to relate to kids,' he says. 'So I speak the same language. Why not?'

5 Relating to the pupils was certainly a challenge. All of them had been excluded from their schools for serious offences. Fighting and swearing came naturally to them – studying didn't! In fact, they seemed less able to concentrate than the average mosquito! Take Shane, for example. He was a troublemaker in a hoody who used to bully, swear and steal. Or Grace, who had 'Me Me Me' written on her T-shirt, a phrase which summed up her brand of egotism quite perfectly. 'I can't be bothered!' was her catchphrase in her old school.

6 Luckily, Beadle got on with the kids, and they got on with him. He didn't try to make them learn in ways that didn't suit them. He took time to talk with them, to hear about their problems and help them identify their talents. Then he planned the best way to boost their confidence and help them achieve their goals. 'Good teaching isn't about being the old bore at the front of the class with a textbook,' he says.

7 His methods may seem strange but Beadle claims they're based on educational theory. And they seem to work. After *The Unteachables*, Shane settled down at school and now wants to be a plumber. 'It's phenomenal,' says his mother. 'He's chilled, a totally different boy.' And Grace, who once threw a wooden pole at a teacher, now gets on well at school and has stopped truanting. Like the others, she's set on getting qualifications so she can realise her dreams.

8 Not all the kids stayed the course; some were chucked off home early on in the series. But the improvement of the others surprised everyone, even the producers. Kids who 'muck about' in class disrupt their own and others' chances of learning. It's a terrible waste of talent. If more teachers follow Beadle's lead and respect their pupils as individuals while setting clear rules and boundaries, maybe, just maybe, school will get a whole lot better for everyone concerned.

Education

→ For exercises 1–5 see pages 54 and 58 in your Students' Book.

1 Complete the sentence with a suitable word. The first letter has been given.

1 I didn't do my homework last night so I've got to stay behind after class as a punishment and do ......*detention*........ .

2 A boy in my class started a fight and now he's been e...................... from the school for good!

3 When we went away on our geography field course, we stayed in special accommodation and eight of us had to sleep in the same d...................... .

4 When you go to your university graduation ceremony, you have to wear a g...................... over your normal clothes.

5 My maths teacher is easy-going but my sports teacher is extremely s......................!

6 We did a really interesting e...................... with nitric acid in science today.

7 Have a look at your t...................... and see what lesson we have next, will you?

8 If you really feel ill, you should tell a member of s...................... and they'll telephone your parents.

2 Choose the correct word to complete the sentences.

1 Do you think you'll *achieve/pass* all your exams?

2 Are you confident you'll *achieve/pass* good grades?

3 If I *fail/miss* English, I'll take the exam again next year.

4 When I leave school, I'm going to *fail/miss* all my friends.

5 My uncle is a *teacher/professor* at a big university.

6 His dad is a school *teacher/professor* .

7 The teacher isn't strict enough – he can't *control/punish* the class.

8 The head will *control/punish* you if he finds out you broke the window!

9 My *notes/grades* aren't good enough for university – I'm really disappointed!

10 I'm going to miss the history lecture today so could you take some *notes/grades* for me?

3 Complete the sentences with the correct form of *take, make* or *do*.

1 If you ....*make*......... an effort, you can finish your project today.

2 The experiment we .... today went all wrong!

3 It'll .... ages to type up all these notes.

4 I'm .... detention so I can't come home now.

5 The teacher warned that if we .... any more noise, we'll get sent out.

6 I know Alice is out but could you .... a message, please?

7 How much progress have you .... this term?

8 Have you .... your homework yet?

4 Complete the sentences with phrasal verbs formed from these two groups.

| fall | catch | get | ~~hand~~ | put | work |

| off | out | up | through | ~~in~~ | behind |

1 I didn't realise we were supposed to ....*hand in*......... our essays today.

2 I've missed a lot of work and I don't know if I'll ever .... with the other students.

3 We .... the party because Dad isn't well.

4 I can't .... where we are on this map.

5 I'm sure I'll .... the test if you give me a hand.

6 He keeps playing truant, which means he's always .... with his studies.

5 Choose the word or phrase that best completes the sentence.

1 She was ..A.. in a small village in Africa and had to walk 10 kilometres to school every day.
   A brought up   **B** grown up

2 Our careers teacher tries to help us decide what we want to ..... for a living.
   A make   **B** do

3 Stop talking and get ..... with your work!
   A in   **B** on

4 They've cut ..... the tree that used to grow in the playground.
   A down   **B** off

5 Our drama group is holding ..... for parts in next term's musical.
   A tests   **B** auditions

Comparative structures

→ For exercises 1–2 see page 55 in your Students' Book.

1 Complete the table.

Adjective /Adverb	Comparative	Superlative
hot	hotter	the hottest
easy		
hard		
carefully		
good/well		
bad/badly		
far		
comfortable		
little		
many		

2 Rewrite the sentences using the words in capitals. Use between two and five words, including the word given.

1 Our first class wasn't as interesting as this one.
LESS
Our first class was .less. interesting .than. this one.

2 The exam was easy enough for us all to pass.
SUCH
It was .... we all passed.

3 I was too slow to catch the bus.
ENOUGH
I wasn't .... the bus.

4 I've never read such a thrilling novel.
THE
This is .... have ever read.

5 It was such a boring lesson I fell asleep.
SO
I was .... fell asleep.

6 If you work harder, you'll get better grades.
THE
The harder .... you'll get.

7 This area is dangerous so children can't play on it.
TOO
This area .... to play on.

8 The weather was so bad we couldn't play outside.
SUCH
It was .... couldn't play outside.

9 His essay was worse than mine.
AS
My essay .... his.

10 She doesn't play basketball as well as me.
THAN
I play .... her.

Determiners

→ For exercises 3–5 see page 59 in your Students' Book.

3 Complete the sentences with *few*, *a few*, *little*, or *a little*.

1 He hasn't studied so there's ....little........ hope of him passing the exam.

2 Can you give me .... more minutes, please?

3 Physics is hard so .... students get A grades in it.

4 Would you like .... more chocolate?

4 Choose the word or phrase that best completes the sentence.

1 *None of/None* us want to do extra homework tonight!

2 Did you have *many/much* trouble finding the information on the internet?

3 Don't buy any more computer paper – we've got *plenty of/plenty* in the box.

4 I'd like to stop and chat but I haven't got *many/ much* time.

5 Unfortunately there were *too little/too few* people willing to pay for the school trip so it was cancelled.

5 Complete the text with <u>one</u> word which best fits each gap.

Hi John!

I've only got a 1) few minutes so this is a very quick note.

It's about our end-of-term party. Good news! Nearly 2) ..... the people we invited are coming - I never dreamt we'd get so 3) ..... refusals!

Anyway, the thing is, with forty guests coming, we need a 4) ..... more food and drink! We've got 5) ..... of bread for sandwiches but we've got very 6) ..... meat or cheese to fill them with. And we've got too 7) ..... cans of fizzy drink - we'll need lots more!

By the way, it seems there's 8) ..... hope at all of hiring a live band to play, so could you bring 9) ..... few CDs? You're a star!

Love

Anna

Use your English

1 Complete the text with <u>one</u> word which best fits each gap.

Education – past and present

Schools have seen a 1) .... great .... deal of change. In the 19th century there were very 2) .... schools, so a 3) .... number of people couldn't read or write. A 4) .... of children worked in factories. Their parents were 5) .... poor to send them to school. Rich boys were 6) .... fortunate. Their parents could afford expensive private schools.

In the last century, it became much 7) .... acceptable for young children to go out to work so the government was able to make education compulsory. Schools were not as good 8) .... they are today. Parents weren't rich 9) .... to pay for good buildings. There was very 10) .... money for books, either. Teachers had 11) .... big classes that they found it hard to manage. To keep discipline, they caned pupils with a wooden stick. The naughtier the kids were, 12) .... harder they were caned! Life was trickier for teachers 13) .... you'd suppose. Some parents thought things were 14) .... when their children went to work, so they attacked teachers. The situation was 15) .... bad in some areas that teachers had to learn boxing in order to defend themselves!

2 Choose the word or phrase that best completes the sentence.

1 The less I have to study, ..C..!
- **A** better
- **B** the best
- **C** the better
- **D** best

2 There were ..... books for me to carry so I left some in the classroom.
- **A** so many
- **B** such a lot
- **C** too many
- **D** few enough

3 My parents aren't ..... keen as yours on paying for the trip.
- **A** as
- **B** such
- **C** very
- **D** too

4 When have we got to ..... in our homework?
- **A** hand
- **B** deliver
- **C** fetch
- **D** put

5 We had far ..... computers in my old school than in this one.
- **A** little
- **B** fewer
- **C** less
- **D** least

6 Gordon is ..... boring person I've ever met!
- **A** the more
- **B** most
- **C** more
- **D** the most

7 If it rains, we'll have to ..... the tennis match.
- **A** put down
- **B** put by
- **C** put across
- **D** put off

8 When the teacher asked for a volunteer, ... of kids put up their hands.
- **A** some
- **B** plenty
- **C** many
- **D** few

9 I can't ..... what this word means.
- **A** work out
- **B** work up
- **C** work in
- **D** work over

10 There's a film on TV but ..... of us want to watch it.
- **A** nobody
- **B** no one
- **C** none
- **D** anyone

11 I've got so far behind with my work it'll be hard to ..... up.
- **A** bring
- **B** let
- **C** make
- **D** catch

12 I've got a great ..... of revision to do.
- **A** number
- **B** lot
- **C** plenty
- **D** deal

13 The teacher will ..... you off if you disturb the lesson.
- **A** put
- **B** tell
- **C** call
- **D** push

14 My brother got ..... all his exams – in fact, he got A grades!
- **A** past
- **B** through
- **C** down
- **D** into

Writing *an essay*

➜ For exercises 1–7 see pages 60–61 in your Students' Book.

1 Read the writing task and answer the questions.

> You've had a class discussion on education and your teacher has asked you to write an essay of 120–180 words, on this topic: *Schooldays are the happiest days of our lives. Do you agree?*

1 Who is going to read your essay?
2 Will your reader expect you to use a neutral/formal or an informal style?
3 Does your reader expect you to:
   – list complaints about your school?
   – describe various events in your life?
   – mention both sides of the argument?
4 Do you agree or disagree with the statement about schooldays? Why? Note down three reasons for your opinions.
5 Think why people might take an opposite view to you. Note down one or two of the arguments they might use.

2 Look at the writing task again. Decide if these ideas agree with the title of the essay or disagree with it. Write them in the correct column below.

1 You have to do what you're told.
2 It's a great place to make friends and see them all the time.
3 Learning new things can be exciting.
4 You may be stuck all day in class with people you don't like.
5 It's hard to sit and listen all day.
6 You don't need to worry about things like money.
7 It's boring having to study subjects you don't like.
8 You've got very few responsibilities.

Reasons to agree	Reasons against

3 Which of the following is not an appropriate way to express an opinion in this essay?

In my opinion, …
As I see it, …
I think/tend to think that …
It's rubbish to say that …
Some people say that … but I don't agree. I believe that …
It's true that … On the other hand, …

4 Which of the following is not a word or phrase that can be used to list similar reasons?

First of all, …
Another point is that …
In addition, …
Furthermore, …
Moreover, …
However, …
Finally, …
In conclusion, …
Lastly, …

5 Here are sections for your essay. Decide where the sections should go on the paragraph plan.

– reservations/why some people might disagree with my opinion
– conclusion
– my opinion
– introduction

> **Paragraph 1** ....
> **Paragraph 2** ....
> **Paragraph 3** ....
> **Paragraph 4** ....

6 Tick the paragraph that you think would make the best introduction to the writing task in Exercise 1.

1 Are schooldays really the best days of our lives? On the whole I think they are, though with some small reservations.
2 It is often said that schooldays are the happiest days of our lives. That's absolute rubbish.
3 Schooldays are the best days of our lives. It's true and I'll tell you why.

7 Now write your answer to the writing task in Exercise 1, using the paragraph plan you made above.

Do you need more practice?
Go to: CD-ROM, Unit 5.

Vocabulary

→ For exercises 1–4 see pages 62–63 in your Students' Book.

1 Complete the table.

Nouns	Adjectives (no negative forms)
care	careful
curve	
glamour	
health	
hunk	
muscle	
skin	
trend	

2 Complete the sentences with a noun or adjective from Exercise 1.

1 Wearing a baseball cap back to front may be considered ....trendy......... at the moment but I think it looks silly!
2 Eating a lot of salt and fat is bad for your ....
3 My sister and I are quite different – I'm a bit plump but she's really ....
4 The actress was wearing a black dress and diamonds and looked extremely ....
5 Dad dressed with a lot of .... this morning because he's got an important interview.
6 Since Ed started lifting weights in the gym, his arms have become really strong and ....

3 Complete the words to label the picture. The first letter has been given.

7 f...........................
1 eyebrow...............
6 s...........................
5 w...........................
4 s...........................
2 f...........................
3 d............ c...............

4 Complete the sentences with the correct form of these verbs.

blame   kid   matter   resist
risk   ruin   waste   ~~worry~~

1 I know it's dangerous but please don't ....worry......... about me. I'll take care not to fall!
2 I know I shouldn't eat so much chocolate but when I'm offered some, I can't .... it!
3 We .... a lot of time trying on clothes that we couldn't afford.
4 It doesn't .... what you look like – I still love you!
5 Wear a suit? Are you ....? There's no way I'll do that!
6 We wanted to party so we .... inviting people round for a barbecue even though it looked like rain.
7 Alice .... me for spilling orange juice on her skirt but it wasn't my fault at all!
8 The bad weather .... our holiday so we came home early.

Reading

1 Read the text and choose the sentence (A–H) that best fits each gap (1–7). There is one extra sentence which you do not need to use.

A I'll tell you a secret.
B After a while I thought, hang on – I feel fine in my body, so is this me or is it them?
C But Kate means what she says and is willing to take legal action against those who don't respect her wishes.
D From the earliest time she can remember, she wanted to be an actress.
E Most people respect her for her down-to-earth attitude, and her actor friends like Johnny Depp (*Pirates of the Caribbean*), love her for it.
F She doesn't diet; she just eats sensibly and gets lots of exercise.
G Some of the people who saw her on screen suggested she had a weight problem.
H The image of her standing, arms out, at the front of the ship is familiar to millions of us.

Body**Talk**

While other actresses battle to look perfect, Kate Winslet has always refused to change. She tells us why she's decided to speak out for real women.

Most leading actresses think airbrushing is the ideal way to maintain the illusion of perfect looks. Kate Winslet does not agree.

Kate is an Oscar-winning movie actress and celebrated beauty. She first came to fame when she starred in the film *Titanic* opposite Leonardo diCaprio. 1) .H.. But Kate believes that today's media is giving us a totally false idea of what a normal woman should look like. This is why, unlike most other celebrities, she refuses to let anyone touch up her photos to remove wrinkles, to zap spots, to make her legs look longer or for any other reason.

Kate's fight against airbrushing is pretty unique in the cosmetics industry. Here, perfecting a model's image by artificial means is common practice. 2) ..... A few years ago she threatened to sue a magazine that used digital imaging to make her look younger. And when she agreed to model for a perfume company, it was only on condition that the company

promised not to airbrush her for their poster campaign.

Kate is clearly extremely comfortable with the way she looks and likes being normal. 'I'm not perfect,' she insists, 'and I don't want to be seen as someone who is. I hate the idea that women in films are perfect because they have some kind of secret beauty that nobody else has. 3) ..... The reason that women in films are perfect is because we've all been through three-and-a-half hours of hair and make-up!'

Kate grew up in a town not far from London. Both her parents were actors. Times were hard but although there wasn't much money around, there was plenty of love. 4) ..... Other kids at school wanted to be air hostesses or hairdressers but acting was the only career she could contemplate. She wasn't star-struck or over-assertive. She just knew what she wanted to do.

It was while making the film *Titanic* that Kate became aware of another Hollywood hang-up – body shape. 5) ..... She didn't agree. She's not skinny, of course, but she's not fat either – just naturally curvy with broad shoulders.

'I didn't think I was overweight at all!' she says. 'I mean I know I'll never be a stick, but in order for me to be really thin, I mustn't eat anything – and I'm not prepared to do that. I've always just been myself, and I thought I looked OK. But all of a sudden people were talking about my body image … something I'd never even thought about before. 6) ..... And at last I realised that it was them!'

Kate thinks it's wrong for women to be forced to conform to an image that is unrealistic and unhealthy. And she is convinced that men don't like ultra-skinny, bony women anyway. Her decision to speak out on such matters surprised a lot of people in the celebrity world, but Kate doesn't care about that. 7) ..... That's why she has become a perfect role model to thousands of women who want to look good without becoming stick thin.

Physical appearance

→ For exercises 1–4 see pages 64 and 68 in your Students' Book.

1 Match the words (1–10) with the definitions (a–j).

1	controversial	a	hole made for wearing jewellery
2	dye		
3	fake	b	become healthy again (for a wound)
4	heal		
5	highlight	c	causing a lot of disagreement and argument
6	infection		
7	ornament	d	cover with a line of colour, to make something stand out
8	piercing		
9	tan	e	darker colour skin caused by exposure to sun
10	view		

f disease in part of the body caused by bacteria

g made to look real in order to deceive people

h object that you keep in a house as a decoration

i opinion

j substance used to change the colour of hair

2 Put the adjectives in brackets in the correct position in the sentences.

1 He's wearing a _short black leather_ jacket. (leather/black/short)

2 I've bought some .... trousers for the party. (baggy/long/fabulous)

3 We got my sister some .... shoes for her birthday. (green/funky/canvas)

4 The actress wore a .... dress for the film premiere. (Chinese/long/silk/beautiful)

5 The tramp was carrying a pair of .... boots in his hands. (rubber/old/dirty)

3 Complete the sentences with these words.

eye   hand   head   leg   neck   ~~tongue~~

1 The actor's name is on the tip of my .... _tongue_ .... I'll remember it in a minute!

2 You've won the lottery? I don't believe it! You're pulling my ....

3 Since Rachel met her new boyfriend, she's had her .... in the clouds.

4 The zip on my jacket keeps sticking. It's a pain in the ....!

5 Keep an .... on that woman. I think she's shoplifting!

6 That suitcase looks heavy! Let me give you a .... with it.

4 Choose the correct verbs to complete the sentences.

1 If you don't think those jeans _fit/suit_ you, try a larger size.

2 You should _carry/wear_ smart clothes if you're going for an interview.

3 John _looks/looks like_ gorgeous when he smiles!

4 Does this tie _match/agree_ this shirt? The colours seem wrong to me.

5 My little brother's only three years old but he can _clothe/dress_ himself.

Conditionals

➔ For exercises 1–5 see pages 65 and 69 in your Students' Book.

1 **Choose the word or phrase that best completes the sentence.**

1 You won't be able to buy those jeans .A. you save.
   A unless   **B** if
2 I'll lend you my jacket ..... you look after it.
   A suppose   **B** provided
3 I'd go to the disco ..... I had something decent to wear.
   A even if   **B** if only
4 Would you like to go to a fashion show, ... you had a ticket of course?
   A on condition that   **B** supposing that
5 I wouldn't wear a suit ..... you paid me!
   A as long as   **B** even if

2 **Complete the sentences with the correct form of the verbs in brackets.**

1 Hurry up! We .... 'll be .... (be) too late for the shops unless we .... (leave) now.
2 I .... (get) some designer trainers if I .... (have) enough money.
3 Suppose you .... (lose) your mobile phone, would you buy the same model of phone again?
4 I .... (wear) a fancy dress costume in the carnival as long as you .... (promise) to do the same.
5 Woollen sweaters .... (always/ shrink) if you .... (wash) them at the wrong temperature.
6 Don't worry! If I .... (see) the jeans you want in the store, I .... (ask) the assistant to put them by for you.

3 **Choose the correct verb form to complete the sentences.**

1 If I *wore/had worn* a T-shirt instead of a sweater, I wouldn't have got so hot.
2 I wouldn't have my tongue pierced if I *were/would be* you.
3 I could ring Trudy if I *didn't lose/hadn't lost* her phone number.
4 You can become a fashion designer if you *have done/ had done* the right kind of training.
5 If you want to look cool, *you don't/don't* borrow your parents' clothes!
6 If I *had/had had* an early night instead of going to the disco, I wouldn't be so tired now.

4 **Complete the sentences with the correct form of the verbs in brackets.**

1 Don't dye your hair unless your mum .... says .... (say) it's okay.
2 If you .... (have) your tongue pierced, it .... (sometimes/hurt) a lot!
3 I .... (not/put) that jacket in the washing machine if I .... (be) you.
4 I'll lend him the money as long as he .... (pay) me back.
5 If I .... (know) it was going to snow, I .... (wear) my boots.
6 Mum says I can go out provided I .... (finish) my homework.

5 **Match the sentence beginnings (1–8) to the sentence endings (a–h). Then write out the sentences in full.**

1 If you hadn't joined the gym,
2 If you were going to hear from her,
3 If you really liked her,
4 If the buses weren't on strike,
5 If you're planning to get a tattoo,
6 If you went to bed very late last night,
7 If you were a bit more sensible,
8 If the shoes don't fit you,

a I wouldn't bother telling your parents.
b you could always get your money back.
c you probably aren't feeling at your best today.
d you would have realised your mistake earlier.
e you wouldn't be so fit.
f you wouldn't have let her down like that.
g you'd have got a letter by now.
h you'd probably have arrived on time.

1 If you hadn't joined the gym you wouldn't be so fit.

Use your English

1 **Rewrite the sentences using the words in capitals. Use between two and five words, including the word given.**

1 I don't think you should buy that sweater.
YOU
If <u>I were you, I would</u> not buy that sweater.

2 The shop assistant spoke softly so I couldn't hear her.
IF
I would have heard the shop assistant
.... louder.

3 Unhealthy eating makes people ill.
UNLESS
People get ill ....
properly.

4 We didn't play tennis because of the rain.
RAINED
If .... we would have played tennis.

5 I didn't win the lottery so I can't buy a car.
ABLE
If I'd won the lottery, I
.... buy a car.

6 I can't finish this work without your help.
UNLESS
I can't finish this work
.... me.

7 Would you come to the party if you didn't have something to do this evening?
FREE
Suppose .... this evening, would you come to the party?

8 She's not working as a model because she got married.
STILL
If she hadn't got married she
.... as a model.

2 **Read the article and choose the best answer, A, B, C or D.**

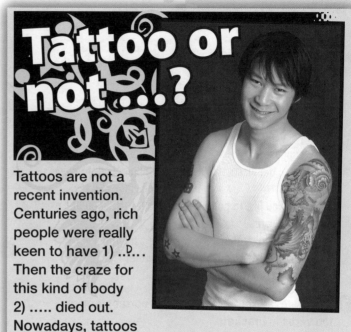

Tattoo or not...?

Tattoos are not a recent invention. Centuries ago, rich people were really keen to have 1) ..D... Then the craze for this kind of body 2) ..... died out. Nowadays, tattoos 3) ..... become trendy again. David Beckham and Jennifer Aniston are just two of the celebrities 4) ..... have them. If you are 5) ..... of getting a tattoo, here is some advice. First, 6) ..... sure that you are old enough. In some countries you have to be 7) ..... least eighteen years old to get a tattoo. The next thing you 8) ..... do is look for a reputable tattoo artist. Make sure 9) ..... in his room is clean and sterile, including the needles and other equipment. You could get a serious skin 10) ..... if the needles are dirty. Then stop and think. The tattoo artist will inject ink deep into your skin. It may feel extremely 11) ..... or if you're lucky, just uncomfortable. Tattoos are permanent 12) ..... you can't change your mind after it's done. Be sure you won't 13) ..... up regretting the decision.

1 A it	**B** that	**C** this	**D** them
2 A ornament	**B** jewellery	**C** decoration	**D** piercing
3 A is	**B** have	**C** will	**D** had
4 A whom	**B** which	**C** who	**D** that
5 A considering	**B** thinking	**C** meaning	**D** wanting
6 A take	**B** do	**C** stay	**D** make
7 A at	**B** in	**C** on	**D** by
8 A ought	**B** would	**C** won't	**D** should
9 A nobody	**B** something	**C** everyone	**D** everything
10 A illness	**B** infection	**C** injection	**D** wound
11 A painful	**B** tearful	**C** hurtful	**D** harmful
12 A although	**B** because	**C** so	**D** as
13 A end	**B** come	**C** give	**D** keep

Writing *a formal letter*

➔ For exercises 1–6 see pages 70–71 in your Students' Book.

1 Read the writing task and answer these questions.

1 Who is going to read your letter?
2 Will your reader expect you to use a neutral/formal or an informal style?

You are living in an English-speaking country. The students at your school have all been sent the following handout. Read the handout and the notes you've written about it. Then write a letter to Mr Storm in 120–150 words, using all your notes.

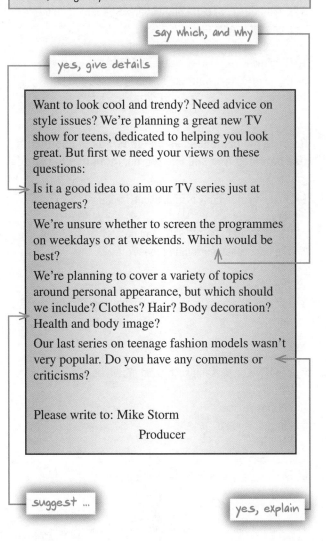

say which, and why

yes, give details

Want to look cool and trendy? Need advice on style issues? We're planning a great new TV show for teens, dedicated to helping you look great. But first we need your views on these questions:

Is it a good idea to aim our TV series just at teenagers?

We're unsure whether to screen the programmes on weekdays or at weekends. Which would be best?

We're planning to cover a variety of topics around personal appearance, but which should we include? Clothes? Hair? Body decoration? Health and body image?

Our last series on teenage fashion models wasn't very popular. Do you have any comments or criticisms?

Please write to: Mike Storm
                 Producer

suggest …

yes, explain

2 What must you say in your letter? Complete this list of points.

1 Say .... and give reasons why.
2 Say whether ....
....
....
....

3 Which of these items would be suitable for your letter? Tick them.

1 Hello there!
2 Dear Mr Storm,
3 I hope you are well.
4 I am writing to give you my ideas on your next TV series for teens.
5 Well, that's it for now.
6 I hope my ideas are helpful.
7 Love and best wishes,
8 Yours sincerely,

4 Which of these phrases are too direct for a formal letter? Rephrase them so that they are more polite.

1 I suggest you include something about body decoration because it's very trendy at the moment.
2 Your last programme was just awful.
3 I think it would be a good idea to have something about body building because boys are interested in that.
4 I insist that you include hair-styling in your list of topics.

5 Tick the words and phrases below that can be used to list points. Put a cross next to those that can be used to start a fresh paragraph or change topic.

1 First, …
2 What's more, …
3 Furthermore, …
4 Turning to your question about …
5 Secondly, …
6 Finally, …
7 As regards …

6 Decide how many paragraphs you need for your letter, and which points to cover in each paragraph. Then complete this plan.

Paragraph 1 Say why I'm writing (to give my comments on the new TV show).
Paragraph 2 ....
Paragraph 3 ....
Paragraph 4 ....
Paragraph 5 ....

7 Now write your answer to the writing task in Exercise 1.

Do you need more practice?
Go to: CD-ROM, Unit 6.

Grammar

1 **Complete the sentences with <u>one</u> word which best fits each gap.**

1 I find physics hard and a bit boring so it's my ………**least**……… favourite subject at school.

2 The more I practise the guitar, …………………… better I get at playing it.

3 What is the …………………… expensive thing you've bought this week?

4 The teacher kept us in school for …………………… long that it was dark by the time we got home!

5 Having your ears pierced isn't nearly as painful …………………… having a tattoo!

6 The denim jacket looks good on you but the leather one looks even …………………… .

7 The mathematics paper was …………………… hard for any of us to understand!

8 I wish I were rich …………………… to dress in the latest designer clothes.

9 Having exams once a term is bad enough but having monthly exams is the …………………… idea I can imagine!

10 Jack is the coolest boy …………………… our class!

2 **Complete the sentences with the correct form of the verbs in brackets.**

1 What a shame! If I ……**had known**…… (know) about last night's party, I …………………… (go)!

2 Unless Dad …………………… (lose) weight soon, he …………………… (not/be able) to wear his suit to the wedding.

3 We …………………… (can) buy some lunch if only we …………………… (have) a bit more money.

4 I …………………… (not/join) their gang, if I …………………… (be) you. They're nothing but trouble!

5 If you …………………… (need) help, just …………………… (give) me a ring.

6 You wouldn't be in so much trouble with your parents now if only you …………………… (tell) them the truth last night.

7 I …………………… (come) to the disco with you provided I …………………… (not get) too much homework.

8 Suppose you …………………… (win) the lottery, how would you spend the money?

9 If I …………………… (stay) out late, my parents …………………… (always/worry) about me.

10 I …………………… (sleep) longer this morning if Mum …………………… (not/wake) me up to answer the phone.

3 **Choose the word or phrase that best completes the sentence.**

1 There are rather .**A**. of students in my English class.
A a large number **B** many
C a great deal **D** a few

2 ….. of my two sisters like school.
A None **B** Few
C Little **D** Neither

3 I've brought ….. sandwiches for lunch. Would you like one?
A a few **B** a lot
C a little **D** an amount

4 I'm sorry but there's very ….. hope you'll pass this exam.
A few **B** much
C little **D** many

5 I've made ….. of extra photocopies so there should be some for everyone.
A a great deal **B** plenty
C some **D** enough

6 Come in! Would you like ….. tea? It's nice and hot.
A any **B** little
C some **D** much

4 **Rewrite the sentences using the words in capitals. Use between two and five words, including the word given.**

1 Studying at midday is impossible because it's so hot.
TOO
It's .**too hot to study**.. at midday.

2 The coat costs more than the jacket.
EXPENSIVE
The jacket isn't …………………… the coat.

3 Take your camera because you might see somebody famous.
CASE
Take your camera …………………… famous.

4 We have never seen such a big crowd before.
WE
This crowd is …………………… seen.

5 I'm too young to get a tattoo.
ENOUGH
I'm …………………… a tattoo.

6 My advice is to apologise to the teacher.
YOU
If I …………………… apologise to the teacher.

7 I can't understand because they speak too quickly.
ME
They speak …………………… understand.

8 Bob was texting his girlfriend in class so the teacher took away his phone.
NOT
The teacher wouldn't have taken away Bob's phone if he …………………… his girlfriend in class.

Vocabulary

5 Complete the sentences with the correct form of the words in capitals.

1 The poem is anonymous, which means that the writer is
........*unknown*........ .   KNOW

2 Police are investigating the mysterious
.... of several horses and suspect
that they've been stolen.   APPEAR

3 My favourite fashion .... was
interviewed on television last night.   DESIGN

4 I hate permed hair – I think it's extremely
....   ATTRACT

5 The tramp was .... dressed in a
second-hand jacket and dirty trousers.   SHABBY

6 Her hair used to be curly but the hairdresser has
.... it for her.   STRAIGHT

7 You look really .... tonight! BEAUTY

8 It's hard to look .... when you've had
to walk two kilometres in the rain!   GLAMOUR

6 Choose the correct word to complete the sentences.

1 If you eat too many sweets, you'll get *freckles/spots/wrinkles*.

2 I'm going to go out tonight and *have/make/do* fun!

3 I'd like to wear this sweater with these trousers but the colours don't *fit/suit/match*.

4 The teacher says I've *had/made/done* a lot of progress this term.

5 Wearing that outfit, you look *like/as/if* a rock star!

6 Did you get good *scores/grades/notes* in the exam?

7 Katherine usually *dresses/wears/carries* in casual clothes.

8 We can't take our books into the exam so we've got to learn everything by *brain/heart/memory*.

7 Choose the word or phrase that best completes the sentence.

1 I don't feel like revising tonight so I've put it ..C.. until tomorrow.
A by
B out
C off
D round

2 I can't remember the name of the restaurant but it's on the ..... of my tongue!
A end
B tip
C point
D edge

3 Oh, stop complaining and ..... with your work.
A get on
B make up
C set off
D take over

4 Don't be such a pain in the .....! You're driving me crazy today!
A back
B foot
C head
D neck

5 It took me ages to work ..... the answer to that maths problem!
A up
B over
C down
D out

6 Why don't you ..... your coat and come out with me?
A pull in
B put on
C get onto
D dress up

7 I forgot I wasn't supposed to mention the party to Ann. I really put my ..... in it, didn't I?
A nose
B tongue
C foot
D mouth

8 I missed a lot of school last week so now I've got to ..... up fast!
A catch
B make
C take
D get

7 Smart stuff

Vocabulary

→ For exercises 1–3 see pages 74–75 in your Students' Book.

1 Choose the phrase that has a similar meaning to the words in italics.

1 My father is going to *experiment* with the car before he buys it.
   A try on   **B** try out

2 John's decided to take part in the 'Young Inventors' competition so he can *demonstrate* his talents as an engineer.
   A show off   **B** show up

3 I want to *discover more information* about the virtual music studio.
   A find out   **B** find for

4 Competing against others in the virtual bobsled *made clear* the best in Duncan's character.
   A brought up   **B** brought out

5 I've never *joined with others to play* an online card game before.
   A taken part of   **B** taken part in

6 Why don't you *try* mixing your own music album?
   A have a go at   **B** have a go in

7 You'll have to *reach* your own conclusions about whether aliens exist or not.
   A come to   **B** come upon

8 With science, you shouldn't *assume* anything.
   A take anything up **B** take anything for granted

2 Complete the sentences with the correct form of these verbs.

view measure ~~improve~~ compete admit
purchase solve compose

1 I'm not very good at physics but I'm determined to ....*improve*.........

2 Detectives .... crimes.

3 They won't .... you without a ticket.

4 They use the Richter Scale to .... how strong earthquakes are.

5 Have you ever .... your own music or written your own lyrics for a song?

6 At the IMAX you can .... the latest *Star Wars* movies.

7 The museum has a shop where you can .... souvenirs.

8 We .... against our friends in the virtual bobsled and we won!

3 Complete the sentences by forming nouns from the words in brackets. Be careful! You may need to use plural forms.

1 The museum welcomes thousands of ....*visitors*........ (visit) every year.

2 The next .... (perform) of *Star Wars* will start in twenty minutes.

3 You don't need a ticket to go into the museum because .... (admit) is free!

4 I really enjoyed all the .... (active) we did when we were pretending to be spies.

5 We enjoyed hearing from the .... (science) who are engaged in building robots.

6 My uncle works as a .... (research) at our local museum.

Reading

1 Read the text and choose the best answer, A, B, C or D.

1 In which museum can you travel back in time in a space vehicle?
   A 1   **B** 2   **C** 3   **D** 4

2 In which place can you hear from real live space travellers?
   A 1   **B** 2   **C** 3   **D** 4

3 In which museum might you be chased by a huge predatory beast?
   A 1   **B** 2   **C** 3   **D** 4

4 In which museum can you encounter fictional strangers from other worlds?
   A 1   **B** 2   **C** 3   **D** 4

5 Which museum can you revisit without charge to see things you missed the first time round?
   A 1   **B** 2   **C** 3   **D** 4

6 Which place can you not visit on Mondays?
   A 1   **B** 2   **C** 3   **D** 4

7 In which museum can you separate truth from fiction and discover the real reason for a historic event?
   A 1   **B** 2   **C** 3   **D** 4

8 Which museum features a fictional vehicle that can fly?
   A 1   **B** 2   **C** 3   **D** 4

9 Which museums would appeal to people interested in the technologies used in the hidden world of espionage?
   A 1 and 3   **B** 2 and 4
   C 1 and 4   **D** 2 and 3

10 In which museum can you get a sense of what living on the Moon might be like?
   A 1   **B** 2   **C** 3   **D** 4

1
Science Museum
Exhibition Road, South Kensington, London SW7 2DD, UK

The Science Museum was founded in 1857 and is renowned for its inspirational exhibitions. Visit *The Science of Aliens*, and get up-close and personal with some classic science-fiction films and props, then come face-to-face with the weird creatures that inhabit Earth, before exploring far-flung planets and stars. Enter the *Alien Worlds* of leading scientists and meet the aliens they have imagined in a unique hands-on environment. *The Science of Spying* is an interactive exhibition. After being recruited as a trainee spy, you can explore the skills and abilities required by real agents and use the latest gadgets that help spies gather information. Then use everything you've learnt to escape from your enemies, before qualifying as a fully trained agent!

Open 10 a.m. – 6 p.m. every day except 24 to 26 December.
Entry is free, but charges apply for the IMAX 3D Cinema, simulators and some special exhibitions.

2
The Natural History Museum
Cromwell Road, London SW7 5BD, UK

The Natural History Museum is home to the largest and most important natural history collection in the world. Come face to face with Tyrannosaurus rex, the most terrifying dinosaur of them all. The giant animatronic model is back, but beware! Its new super-senses might mean you're next on its list of victims .... Marvel at the power of its huge jawbone and 15-centimetre-long teeth. Inspect dinosaur skeletons and sort the facts from the myths about why dinosaurs died out. Experience what an earthquake feels like when you enter the Kobe Supermarket earthquake machine and discover what happens when a volcano erupts.

Entry is free! Open daily 10:00 – 17:50, Sundays included. Closed 24–26 December. Last admission is at 17:30.

3
THE NATIONAL MOTOR MUSEUM
Beaulieu, Hampshire SO42 7Z, UK

Take a trip in a space-age pod as you experience *Wheels*, a dark ride through motoring history. Travel through time from the dawn of man and the first stone-age wheels to a vision of what the cars of the future may look like. Learn about key events in the last 100 years of motoring. View some of the glamorous – and lethal – vehicles featured in the James Bond films. See the gadgets that make up 007's secret world! Also on show is the famous magical flying car, *Chitty Chitty Bang Bang*, from the book of the same name written by Ian Fleming, author of the James Bond stories. This car is the star of one of the best loved family films of all time.

Admission Prices: Adult: £16.25; Youth: £9.25. Come back for FREE if you don't have time to view everything. Open every day 10 a.m. until 6.00 p.m. from end of May to September and from 10 a.m. until 5.00 p.m. from October to end of May. Closed Christmas Day.

4
National Space Centre
Exploration Drive, LE4 5NS Leicester, UK

Opened to the public on 30 June 2001, the Centre is devoted to space science and astronomy. Learn what it takes to become an astronaut and see the rockets that take humans into space. Experience what it would be like to live in a lunar base in the year 2025. Events at the Centre include interviews with astronauts like Buzz Aldrin, the second man to walk on the Moon, and actors and characters from the *Star Wars* films. At our *Rise of the Robot* events you can meet the scientists who build robots, then build your own robot and watch it compete with others in the Combat Zone.

Open: Tue–Sun 10.00–17.00. Last admission: 3.30 p.m. Workshops, demonstrations and competitions free to ticket holders. Admission: £8.50–£42.00. Credit Cards Accepted.

Science and technology

→ For exercises 1–4 see pages 76 and 80 in your Students' Book.

1 Complete the sentences with these words.

virtual   online   website   ~~screen~~   download
chat room   mouse   keyboard

1 The sunlight is reflecting off the ....**screen**........ of my computer so I can't read what's written there.
2 If you move the .... with your hand and press the button, a flashing symbol called a 'cursor' will appear on your computer.
3 Never mind if you can't actually go to the museum. Turn on the computer and you can take a .... tour.
4 All the letter buttons on my .... are wearing out so they're really hard to read.
5 When I can't go out, I turn on my computer and talk to people in a ....
6 Which .... do I need to go to if I want to find information about robots?
7 Not all of our computers are connected to the internet yet but they'll all be .... by next year.
8 You need to .... word processing software onto the computer if you want to write essays on it.

2 Complete the table.

Area	Person
1 science	scientist
2 mathematics	
3 astronomy	
4 chemistry	
5 geology	
6 engineering	
7 physics	
8 biology	

3 Choose the correct words to complete the sentences.

1 If I move the computer to my bedroom, I have to remember to .**B**. it in before I can switch on.
  A wire   **B** plug
2 I managed to ..... a great game from the internet for free!
  A download   **B** crash
3 The mobile phone is a modern hand-held ..... .
  A machine   **B** device
4 I like science classes but my laboratory ..... always go wrong!
  A trials   **B** experiments
5 Do you know the name of the scientist who ..... penicillin?
  A discovered   **B** invented
6 If you ..... the internet, you can find interesting information on all kinds of topics.
  A survey   **B** surf
7 Engineers are ..... research into greener ways to design cars.
  A dealing   **B** conducting
8 Make sure you ..... the correct procedure when you set up your new computer.
  A follow   **B** set

4 Complete the sentences with matching items from these lists.

inter   ~~high~~   soft   web   hard   net

drive   ware   page   ~~tech~~   work   active

1 My dad's company manufactures ....**high-tech**....... gadgets, like satellite navigation systems for cars.
2 The computers we have in school are on a ...., which means they are all interconnected.
3 If you press that .... button on your TV, you can play online games for free!
4 The computer teacher showed us how to build our own ...., with photos of ourselves and stories about our lives.
5 You can't do anything on a computer unless you have some kind of basic .... like a word-processing programme, for example.
6 Computers, mobile phones and digital cameras all have a ...., which is a storage device for storing encoded data.

The passive

→ For exercises 1–5 see pages 77 and 81 in your Students' Book.

Watch out!

Use 'by + a name/noun/pronoun' to say *who* was the agent of an action.
Use 'with' to say *which object* was used.
For example:
The scientist was shot by his wife.
The scientist was shot with a revolver.

1 Complete the sentences with the correct passive tense form of the verbs in brackets.

1 Oh no, look! The museum ....is closed........ (close).
2 A new satellite .... (just/send) into space.
3 The experiment .... (complete) earlier today.
4 .... (the machine/repair) by next week?
5 The scientist gave away the secret while he .... (interview) on TV.
6 The police discovered that the computers .... (steal).

2 Choose the sentences that are in the active and rewrite them in the passive.

1 A new planet has been discovered recently.
2 They are showing visitors round the new exhibit.
3 The bridge was designed by Isambard Kingdom Brunel.
4 Nuclear scientists were carrying out the test.
5 Nobody can have stolen the chemicals.
6 She was attacked with a knife.
7 They must do the experiment with care.
8 Somebody made us clear up the broken test tubes.
9 They let us try out the new computers.
10 I was given a brochure about the museum.

3 Choose the word or phrase that best completes the sentence.

1 The computer I bought was faulty so ..A..
   A I was given a refund.
   B a refund was given to me.
2 The vacuum cleaner needs .....
   A to empty it.
   B emptying.
3 Crick and Watson discovered the secrets of DNA so .....
   A the Nobel Prize was awarded to them.
   B they were awarded the Nobel Prize.
4 Students ..... to use the photocopier.
   A aren't let
   B aren't allowed

4 Complete the second sentence so that it means the same as the first one.

1 Why don't we get someone to fix our computer?
   Why don't we have *our computer fixed*?
2 My car needed servicing so I took it to a garage.
   I took my car to a garage to have ....
3 He's going for an eye test tomorrow.
   He's going to get .... tomorrow.
4 Someone stole my dad's mobile phone last night.
   My dad had .... last night.
5 Someone is checking the car tyres for me.
   I'm getting ....
6 Has someone called your name yet?
   Has .... called yet?

5 Put the words in the correct order to make sentences.

1 shopping. / had / while / He / stolen / was / wallet / he / his
2 done / get / in / managed / the / time. / to / We / work
3 don't / engraved /your / have / initials / mobile / on / phone? / Why / you / your
4 cut. / get / hair / her / ought / She / to
5 your / had / haven't / repaired? / watch / Why / you
6 Did / get / your / last / you / night? / photo / taken

Use your English

1 Complete the text with <u>one</u> word which best fits each gap.

You 1) .... **have** .... probably read about homes that 2) .... powered by the sun, or about robotic dogs that have 3) .... designed to run and bark. But do you understand how it all works? If you find science difficult, a book 4) .... just been published which might just help you. In *Terrific Technology*, the science behind all kinds of amazing inventions 5) .... clearly explained. The book 6) .... written as a novel. A teenage boy mucks about in class. As a punishment, he is 7) .... to do a science project. And his teacher insists he's got to get 8) .... finished in just six weeks. He isn't particularly interested in technology – in fact he is mystified 9) .... it! But he discovers a lot from his project – and so do we, the readers of the book. We learn how lasers can 10) .... used to make CDs. In future, although it's not certain, lasers 11) .... also be used by dentists. This would be fantastic because nobody would need to 12) .... their teeth drilled ever again! *Terrific Technology* is a great book. Study it, and your brain 13) .... certainly be exercised!

2 Read the text and choose the best answer, A, B, C or D.

Every day millions 1) ..A.. people sit at home and 2) ..... their computers. At some point, most of them will 3) ..... online. Some people 4) ..... the internet for specific information. Others 5) ..... newspaper articles or recipes for meals. Many access the internet in 6) ..... to chat to friends – or make new ones. Teenagers used to 7) ..... on mobile phones to contact people. Not any more! Now they go to online 8) ..... like *Bebo*, *MySpace* and *Facebook*. On Bebo, for example, 9) ..... can upload music, videos and photos onto their personal webpages, press a button, and send them to their friends. *Facebook* provides free 10) ..... so you can write your own music. But it's not just humans 11) ..... have their own websites. Dogs who want to 12) ..... to each other online through their owners can log on to *Dogster*. Hundreds of dogs have 13) ..... their pictures and diaries posted there already!

1	**A** of	**B** in	**C** on	**D** and
2	**A** plug in	**B** switch on	**C** turn off	**D** set up
3	**A** come	**B** do	**C** go	**D** put
4	**A** look	**B** see	**C** view	**D** search
5	**A** record	**B** open	**C** download	**D** enter
6	**A** hope	**B** effort	**C** case	**D** order
7	**A** ring	**B** rely	**C** calls	**D** utilise
8	**A** sites	**B** areas	**C** screens	**D** spaces
9	**A** doers	**B** makers	**C** liners	**D** users
10	**A** hardware	**B** ironware	**C** software	**D** glassware
11	**A** which	**B** they	**C** that	**D** who
12	**A** chat	**B** discuss	**C** speak	**D** debate
13	**A** been	**B** had	**C** made	**D** sent

Writing *a review*

→ For exercises 1–6 see pages 82–83 in your Students' Book.

1 Read the writing task and answer the questions.

You see this announcement in a teenage magazine:

Send us a review of an action/adventure or spy movie. We'll publish the best reviews in our magazine. In your review you'll need to outline the plot of the movie, describe any spectacular stunts or high-tech gadgets and say whether you think the movie would appeal to most teenagers.

Write your review in 120–180 words.

1 What kind of magazine are you writing for? How old are the readers?
2 Will your readers expect you to use a very formal style, or a semi-formal/informal style?
3 What kind of movie are you asked to write about? Which will you choose?
4 Here are some of the topics you must include in your review. Which have we forgotten?
– whether the movie would appeal to teenagers
– the gadgets
– ? …
– ? …
5 Note down the plot of your movie in three or four sentences. Have you used present tenses to describe a plot?
6 Have you made a note about any stunts or gadgets used in the movie?

2 Read the review for *Casino Royale* and mark where you think each paragraph should start. Include an introduction and a conclusion.

3 These words and phrases are often used in reviews. Underline them in the *Casino Royale* review.

brilliant
excellent
In one scene, … In another, …
This is a … movie and is/is not suitable for …
If you're looking for a movie full of …, you'll love it!

FILM REVIEW   **RATING ★★★★★**

Casino Royale

Casino Royale is a spy film and is part of the James Bond series. It stars Daniel Craig as the first blond Bond. The plot is brilliant. Bond is sent to Madagascar, where he finds out about a group of terrorists. He is ordered to defeat their banker in a game of cards at a casino. He falls in love with his assistant and promises to leave the secret service for her. But she betrays him. There are fewer gadgets than in previous Bond movies, and this makes the whole thing more realistic. Bond's incredible Aston Martin is featured, of course, and Bond carries his usual gun. The stunts are excellent. In one scene, a police car is thrown high into the air by a moving aeroplane. In another, Bond's Aston Martin is made to roll over seven times while being driven at high speed. This is a tough, violent movie and is definitely not suitable for kids under twelve. But if you're over thirteen and you're looking for a movie full of action and suspense, you'll love it!

4 Here is one possible paragraph plan for your review in Exercise 1. Complete it.

Paragraph 1 (Introduction) name and type of film, main actors/characters
Paragraph 2 ……………………
Paragraph 3 Short description of stunts/gadgets (present tenses, maybe some passives)
Paragraph 4 (Conclusion) Whether the movie is suitable for teens and why.

5 Now write your answer to the writing task in Exercise 1. Do not write about *Casino Royale*!

Do you need more practice?
Go to: CD-ROM, Unit 7.

8 Eat right, stay fit!

Vocabulary

➜ For exercises 1–2 see pages 84–85 in your Students' Book.

1 Choose the correct preposition to complete the sentences.

1 I'd like to introduce you *at/to* the chef.
2 I did all the cooking *by/on* my own.
3 Can you turn me *in/into* a decent cook?
4 Jenny thinks she's the coolest girl *in/at* town!
5 My father left school *on/at* sixteen and went to work in a restaurant.
6 If Ben bunks *off/out of* work again, they'll fire him!
7 The boss accused Fiona *for/of* stealing.
8 I had eaten half the cake when, *at/to* my horror, I found a dead spider inside!
9 That hamburger was made *from/by* the best beef available.
10 I didn't think *Can't cook, won't cook* would be popular but it's taken the country *by/for* storm!

2 Complete the sentences with the correct form of these verbs.

battle   campaign   concentrate   decrease   improve
accuse   ~~persuade~~   survive   promote   run

1 His parents ...... **persuaded** ...... him to take a job as a waiter during the holidays.
2 If I'm very hungry, I find it impossible to .... on studying.
3 Tourists no longer come to this town so the number of restaurants has ....
4 Jamie's doing a series of TV interviews to .... his next show.
5 The customers .... the restaurant owner of overcharging them.
6 I had to eat a meal my brother cooked last night and I only just ....!
7 The man next door earns a good salary because he .... a chain of restaurants.
8 We were very short of staff last night so we had to .... to get everyone served.
9 My cooking used to be awful but I think it has .... recently.
10 My best friend is a vegetarian and she's always .... against cruelty to animals.

Reading

1 Read the article. Match the questions (1–14) with the paragraphs (A–F).

Which paragraph mentions

1 accepting a prize and giving credit to another person?   C
2 giving up spending time with friends to follow a passion?   .....
3 learning techniques that will be useful later?   .....
4 leaving one country in order to live permanently in another?   .....
5 finally becoming a Grand Prix champion?   .....
6 spending a great deal on something that wasn't new?   .....
7 receiving a formal written offer of work?   .....
8 realising that a certain type of behaviour would have bad results?   .....
9 not wanting to stand about the town wasting time?   .....
10 not wishing to be admired too much for one's personality?   .....
11 changing jobs in order not to work the same hours every day?   .....
12 spending enormous time and energy getting ready for a competition?   .....
13 discovering a natural talent for the first time?   .....
14 being persuaded to approach a possible future employer?   .....

A SPORTING HERO

A

He's young, he's charismatic – and he's a champion racing driver! Welcome to the world of Lewis Hamilton, one of the newest kids on the block in the world of Formula 1 racing. Lewis is F1's first mixed-race driver. His father, Anthony, who has been a huge influence on his life, is the son of an immigrant who left the Caribbean to come and settle in the UK; his mum, Carmen, is white. He was also the youngest driver to be offered a contract with McClaren's Young Driver's Racing Team – at the age of just thirteen!

B

It all started when Lewis was on holiday in Spain and decided to have a go at karting. Karts are low-framed vehicles with small wheels and engines and are only driven for recreation. He loved the whole experience! And he knew he was good at it, too. The techniques you need to drive at speed and win a race seemed to come naturally to him. His dad realised how passionate his son was about the hobby so when they got back to the UK, he paid £1,000 to buy Lewis a second-hand kart of his own. It was a huge sum of money for him because he had quite a low-paid job working for the London Underground. But it wasn't wasted. Every weekend the father and son drove out to various kart races where Lewis gradually picked up the skills that would one day make him famous.

C

Of course it's hard to keep up a social life when you spend all your free time going racing. But Lewis didn't mind. He loved his hobby and it filled his life. He didn't want to hang around the streets anyway – he wasn't that kind of boy. And his father wouldn't have approved of it either; he was determined Lewis should make the most of life and take advantage of the opportunities that came his way. He was prepared to make sacrifices for his son – when his boss at the Underground refused to give him time off to take Lewis to races, he resigned and got a new job with more flexible hours. Lewis is the first to acknowledge how much his dad has done for him, which is why he dedicated his first Grand Prix trophy to him.

D

It was his dad who talked Lewis into approaching his future boss at McClaren, Ron Dennis. Lewis had just become Britain's youngest Junior Kart Champion and was invited to an award ceremony. Urged on by his dad, he took the chance to go and speak to Dennis. Three years later, after hearing about all the kart races he had won, Dennis rang Lewis up and invited him to join the Young Driver's Programme. His success quickly led to a contract with a Formula 1 team.

E

Lewis's first Grand Prix was in Australia. His programme of training before the race shows just how committed he is to his sport. It lasted six months. He did two hours of physical training every morning. This was followed by three or four hours of work with his engineers, finding out more about the car he was to drive. Then he put in another three hours of training in the afternoon. By the time he got home every night, he was exhausted. In spite of all his efforts, he didn't win the race. That long-awaited victory came in Canada, in 2007.

F

Lewis is wise enough to know that joining the high life and having luxury yachts and celebrity girlfriends would ruin his career. He is hard-working and determined, personality traits he says he gets from both his parents, whom he clearly adores. He's got the kind of character that makes a great example for other young people, but he doesn't want to be looked up to as a role model. All he wants is to be the greatest racing champion of the world!

Food

→ For exercises 1–5 see pages 86 and 90 in your Students' Book.

1 **Complete the sentence with a suitable word. The first letter has been given.**

1 Some celebrity pop stars and actors employ a ....chef......... to cook all their meals for them.
2 Do you want still water or do you prefer it f........................?
3 Just because food is healthy and n........................, it doesn't mean it tastes good!
4 I want to make spaghetti bolognese but I don't know how to cook it and I can't find a r........................ anywhere!
5 Mmm! That food tasted really d........................!
6 Beef and onions are two of the i........................ you'll need if you want to make hamburgers.
7 You'll ruin your health if you eat nothing but j........................ food.
8 Since Mum went up to stay with Grandma, our d........................ has consisted of fast food followed by more fast food!

2 **Choose the word that best completes the sentence.**

1 Would you like to .B. your meal now?
   A book   **B** order
2 Can I have a ..... of your Cola? I'm so thirsty!
   A sip   **B** swallow
3 Can I have the ....., please? I'd like to see it before I pay up.
   A tip   **B** bill
4 Can I have cheese and biscuits for dessert? I prefer ..... food to sweet stuff.
   A tasty   **B** savoury
5 Help! This meat is so ..... I can't get my knife through it.
   A tough   **B** hard

3 **Rearrange the letters to make words that match the definitions.**

1 It's a round, green vegetable, about the size of a football. (gbcabea) ...._cabbage_........
2 It's a yellow prickly fruit and has hard green leaves at one end. (ppaenielp) ....
3 It's a common dairy product. (seehec) ....
4 It's meat from a farm animal. (blma) ....
5 It swims in the sea. (anmlso) ....
6 It's a round fruit that goes red when it's ripe. (hpace) ....

4 **Complete the sentences with these verbs.**

go   do   cut   ~~give~~   make   put   run   wash

1 I must ....give......... up eating sweets because they're giving me spots!
2 You do the cooking and I'll .... up.
3 Here! Let me help you .... up your apron.
4 Put the milk in the fridge or it will .... off.
5 Mum and Dad always .... on weight when we go on holiday.
6 Oh no! We've .... out of Cola and the shops are shut now.
7 You should .... down on the amount of salt you eat.
8 There was no food in the cupboard so he had to .... do with a cup of coffee.

5 **Complete the sentences with a suitable preposition.**

1 I couldn't get a seat near my friends for the match, so I sat ....on.......... my own.
2 I've been running and now I'm really .... of breath.
3 The teacher .... charge of our football team used to play professionally.
4 I quite like fast food but I prefer home cooking .... the whole.
5 The phone in the restaurant was .... of order.
6 The chef warned me I was .... danger of burning the restaurant down.
7 I thought the meal would be fantastic but it was nothing .... of the ordinary.
8 If you don't wash your hands before handling food, you put your health .... risk.

Gerunds and infinitives

→ For exercises 1–4 see pages 87 and 91 in your Students' Book.

1 **Choose the correct form to complete the sentences.**

1 It's easy *understanding/to understand* why so many people like Italian food.
2 I'm fed up with *doing/to do* gym every day.
3 *Play/Playing* football is my favourite activity.
4 I must give up *eating/to eat* junk food.
5 Do you fancy *coming/to come* to play basketball?
6 I'm tired of *eating/to eat* the same things every day.
7 The sports teacher made me *stay/to stay* behind and practise.
8 You can't avoid to *get/getting* out of breath when you do sport.
9 I was amazed *to see/seeing* footballer David Beckham in our town.
10 My parents won't *to let/let* me take part in motor sports.

2 **Complete the sentences with the correct form of the verbs in brackets.**

1 I persuaded John .... *to come* .... (come) to the match with me.
2 He's really bad at .... (get up) in the morning.
3 As we went into the restaurant we could see the chef .... (prepare) meals in the kitchen.
4 If you want to be good at sport, you have to spend a lot of time .... (train).
5 I've agreed .... (wash up) every night this week!
6 What the coach said made the team .... (try) harder.
7 I'd like to .... (take part) in the Olympics when I'm older.
8 We're looking forward .... (eat) in the new restaurant.
9 They won't let us .... (help) with the barbecue.
10 We're not allowed .... (walk) on the green.

3 **Choose the correct verb form to complete the sentences.**

1 He stopped work *having/to have* a sandwich.
2 He stopped *having/to have* lunch in the cafeteria because he didn't like the food.
3 I remember *buying/to buy* the lemons but I don't know where I've put them!
4 Yes, I did remember *buying/to buy* the lemons. Here they are!
5 If you want to lose weight, try *eating/to eat* less chocolate!
6 I know you're not very hungry, but try *eating/to eat* a little soup and you'll soon feel stronger!
7 I regret *telling/to tell* you bad news, but the match has just been cancelled.
8 I regret *telling/to tell* John the secret because he's bound to tell somebody else.
9 After studying catering, James went on *being/to be* a chef.
10 If you go on *being/to be* silly, you'll get sent out of the class!

4 **Choose the word or phrase that best completes the sentence.**

1 If you want to get fit, I suggest ..A.. more exercise.
 A (that) you take **B** you to take
2 I'd advise ..... wild fungi unless you're sure they're safe.
 A you not to eat **B** you not eating
3 I asked the doctor about my swollen ankle and he advised me against ..... sport for a week.
 A to play **B** playing
4 We need to be at the stadium in half an hour so I suggest ..... now.
 A leaving **B** to leave
5 I'd recommend you ..... some kind of sport.
 A do **B** doing
6 I suggest ..... anybody about our plans.
 A not to tell **B** that we don't tell

Use your English

> → For exercises 1–3 see pages 86–87 and 90–91 in your Students' Book.

1 Choose the word or phrase that best completes the sentence.

1 It's easy ..C.. a court at the local tennis club.
A that you book   B for booking
C to book   D book

2 He managed to avoid ..... the other competitors.
A to run into   B that he ran into
C run into   D running into

3 Mum thinks I spend too much time ..... football.
A on watch   B watching
C to watch   D for watching

4 I think ..... is really boring!
A cooking   B to cook
C cook   D about cooking

5 We've been forbidden ..... on the ice.
A skating   B to skate
C that we skate   D skate

6 You can't make ..... the team!
A me to join   B me join
C that I join   D me joining

7 Lewis Hamilton signed autographs before ..... a TV interview.
A do   B that he did
C to do   D doing

8 I don't fancy ..... that!
A to eat   B that I eat
C eating   D eat

9 I'd recommend ..... the training video.
A watching   B to watch
C watch   D about watching

10 Could you ..... me what to do before the match?
A suggest   B propose
C advise   D recommend

2 Choose the word or phrase that best completes the sentence.

1 This butter tastes strange. I think it's ..C.. .
A gone up   B gone under
C gone off   D gone down

2 I'd like to ..... a table for four people for tonight, please.
A order   B get
C rent   D book

3 Don't ..... all the coffee! I might want a cup later.
A fill up   B use up
C give up   D run up

4 The service was excellent so don't forget to leave the waiter a/an ..... .
A bill   B order
C gift   D tip

5 The charity organisers are going to ..... a party for their helpers.
A host   B invite
C guest   D summon

6 Have you got a ..... for cooking spaghetti carbonara?
A receipt   B menu
C card   D recipe

7 Emma used to be skinny but she's ..... weight now, thank goodness.
A put up   B put over
C put by   D put on

8 The kitchens were closed because of the poor standards of ..... .
A health   B hygiene
C diet   D fitness

9 Dad's got so fat he can't ..... his trousers!
A make up   B size up
C do up   D take up

10 My brother's working as a ..... in the local Chinese restaurant.
A chief   B kitchen
C chef   D cooker

3 Rewrite the sentences using the words in capitals. Use between two and five words, including the word given.

1 We can't play on this pitch because it's frozen.
IMPOSSIBLE
It's .impossible to play. on this pitch because it's frozen.

2 I don't think you should go swimming with that bad cold.
ADVISE
I wouldn't .... with that bad cold.

3 They thought I was the person who had broken the trampoline.
ACCUSED
They .... the trampoline.

4 Mum gave me permission to light the barbecue.
LET
Mum .... the barbecue.

5 Why don't we go to the ice rink tomorrow?
SUGGEST
I .... to the ice rink tomorrow.

6 He hasn't smoked for a year.
GAVE
He .... a year ago.

Writing *a report*

→ For exercises 1–7 see pages 92–93 in your Students' Book.

1 **Read the writing task and answer the questions.**

Your school is planning to start a Health and Fitness Club. Your head teacher has asked you to write a report, giving suggestions about the range of activities it could offer, when and where the Club should meet and how to encourage pupils to come to the Club.
Write your report in 120–180 words.

1 Who is going to read your report?
2 Will the reader expect you to use a neutral style or an informal, chatty style?

2 **Which of these points should you <u>not</u> include in your report? Cross them out.**

– suggestions about ways to advertise the Club
– suggestions about/descriptions of what people could do in the Club
– your opinion about whether pupils should pay to join the Club
– suggestions about when and where the Club should meet
– your opinion about whether your school needs a Club or not

3 **Which points from Exercise 2 could you put under these main headings? Write them in.**

• **Activities to offer**

    ....

• **Place and time**

    ....

• **Recruiting members**

    ....

Check!

Have you used clear headings?
Have you given a reason for each suggestion?
Have you used an impersonal style?

4 **How should you start your report? Choose the best option from those below:**

1

Dear Sir
Here are some suggestions for our new Health and Fitness Centre.

2

To: The head teacher
Subject: The Health and Fitness Club
Introduction: The purpose of this report is to make suggestions for our new Club.

3

To whom it may concern:
Can I begin by saying how pleased I am to hear about our new Club.

5 **Which of these would make the best conclusion?**

1 I hope all this will be useful to you,
  Yours sincerely
  . . .
2 I hope the suggestions in this report will help to make our Club successful.
3 Finally, please let me know if you need any other information. Good luck!

6 **Write full sentences, using these prompts.**

1 I suggest/Club/meet/at least twice a week because it/be/important/exercise regularly/get fit.
2 I recommend/put posters/our school noticeboards so everyone/read about the Club.
3 I think we/offer a range of activities, both indoor and outdoor, so we/sure that there/be/something for everyone.

7 **Now write your answer to the writing task in Exercise 1.**

Do you need more practice?
Go to CD-ROM, Unit 8.

Grammar

1 Complete the text with <u>one</u> word which best fits each gap.

Have you ever hung clothes out 1)..........in.......... the garden and returned a short while later to find they've 2)........................ soaked by the rain? It's a situation many of us have experienced. But the problem 3)........................ have been solved! British university student Oliver MacCarthy 4)........................ just thought up a brilliant way to keep your clothes dry – smart clothes pegs! Oliver was set a project 5)........................ his tutor. He had to design a smart new household object. Oliver 6)........................ inspired by his own experience with soggy jeans, and came 7)........................ with the idea of a clothes peg that can predict the weather! His invention works 8)........................ this. The bag that holds the pegs is manufactured so that it can sense changes in air pressure. Electrical signals 9)........................ sent from this bag to metal strips on the household pegs. If rain 10)........................ predicted within the next half hour, the peg locks itself. This 'lock-down' prevents the washing from 11)........................ hung on the line. Unfortunately the system doesn't include 12)........................ way of protecting clothes from the rain once they are hung out!

2 Put the words in the correct order to make sentences.

1 cleaned/get/jacket/must/soon/that/You
2 finished/get/her/homework/just/managed/on/She/time/to
3 don't/dyed/get/hair/like/mine?/Why/you/your
4 got/has/have/He/his/repaired/to/watch
5 a/am/arm!/getting/heart/I/my/of/on/tattoed/thinking
6 had/her/in/market/purse/She/stolen/the/yesterday.
7 got/have/I've/taken up/these/to/jeans.
8 have/his/When/he/last/tested?/eyes/did

3 Choose the word or phrase that best completes the sentence.

1 I'm really looking forward .C. in the football match tomorrow.
   A to play
   B playing
   C to playing
   D play

2 I'm trying ..... this machine to work!
   A getting
   B to get
   C to getting
   D get

3 My poor neighbours ..... while they were on holiday.
   A had their flat robbed
   B robbed their flat
   C had robbed their flat
   D got robbed their flat

4 I recommend you ..... our local sports centre.
   A to join
   B to joining
   C that join
   D join

5 It's not worth ..... a lot of money on a computer game that's out of date.
   A spending
   B that you spend
   C to spend
   D you to spending

6 The dentist says I've got to .....
   A have taken out a tooth.
   B have a tooth taken out.
   C take out a tooth.
   D have him taken out a tooth.

7 My parents won't let ..... alcohol.
   A me to drink
   B that I drink
   C me drinking
   D me drink

8 He was made ..... for the damage to the tennis court.
   A paying
   B pay
   C to pay
   D paid

Vocabulary

4 **Choose the correct words to complete the sentences.**

1 My brother's an engineer and he's always coming up with ideas for crazy new *discoveries/inventions*.
2 A pocket calculator is a very useful little *gadget/appliance*.
3 I don't think scientists should be allowed to *investigate/experiment* on animals.
4 Pharmacists have been *searching/researching* the effects of certain medicines.
5 The waiter's forgotten to add our coffees to the *bill/tip*!
6 I'm going to *download/collect* music off the computer.
7 You idiot! The machine won't work unless you *switch/plug* it in!
8 Mum says I should eat more fruit and vegetables and give up eating *junk/rubbish* food.
9 Sophie spends hours *swimming/surfing* the internet.
10 Let's go to the party tonight and have a *fun/laugh*!

5 **Choose the word or phrase that best completes the sentence.**

1 Oh no! We've run ..C.. milk! Shall I go and get some?
  A down on
  B away with
  C out of
  D up to
2 My dad wanted to be a footballer when he was at school but he ended ..... as a chef.
  A off
  B up
  C out
  D over
3 As people get older, they often ..... on weight.
  A put
  B get
  C set
  D let
4 The comedian's jokes went ..... well with the audience.
  A off
  B in
  C down
  D well
5 This is secret. It's nothing to ..... with you!
  A interest
  B make
  C concern
  D do
6 Well, our team didn't come last, ... any rate!
  A in
  B at
  C for
  D by

6 **Read the text and choose the best answer, A, B, C or D.**

CYBERFASHION

Most of us own modern 1) ..B.. like mobile phones, or digital cameras. We carry them round in our pockets, or attach them to our bodies. But not for much longer! Designers have now 2) ..... in integrating tiny bits of technology directly into our clothing. 3) ..... fact 'cyberfashion' is the latest trend! One example, the Musical Jacket, is already in the shops. This jacket is silk. It 4) ..... controlled by a keyboard, also manufactured from fabric, which is connected to a tiny device 5) ..... plays music. At present, you 6) ..... to touch a shoulder pad to hear the music. But in future, you'll be able to operate 7) ..... device just by turning your wrist or walking! For athletes, scientists have 8) ..... a smart shirt which measures your heart rate, body temperature and respiration rate! 9) ..... the most romantic piece of cyberfashion must be the Heartthrob Brooch. This item of jewellery, made from diamonds and rubies, has two miniature transmitters. They 10) ..... the brooch glow in time to the beating of its wearer's heart. If you 11) ..... someone gorgeous, your heart will beat faster – and your brooch will 12) ..... everyone know how you feel!

		A	B	C	D
1		machines	gadgets	instruments	tools
2		enabled	managed	succeeded	resulted
3		In	For	By	As
4		was	has	can	is
5		that	it	who	whose
6		must	should	have	could
7		a	any	that	the
8		invented	dreamed	discovered	imagined
9		Although	However	Despite	While
10		cause	force	make	bring
11		met	will meet	are meeting	meet
12		let	allow	permit	admit

9 Shop around

Vocabulary

→ For exercises 1–3 see pages 96–97 in your Students' Book.

1 Complete the sentences with the correct noun.

accessories   appeal   ~~label~~   lifestyle   logo
product   symbol   victim

1 If you look at the ....label.......... on that
   jacket, you can see where it was made.
2 She wears the most fashionable styles even if she
   looks awful in them – she's a real fashion
   ....!
3 The new design of jeans has a very wide
   .... for teenagers.
4 My mum's bought a dress to wear to the wedding but
   she needs matching .... to go with
   it.
5 Tony had a watch with a famous
   .... engraved on it so it must have
   cost a fortune.
6 He wore a yellow ribbon as a ....
   of support for a charitable cause.
7 Millionaires can buy anything they want so they lead
   an extremely lavish ....
8 If there's a manufacturing fault in a particular
   ...., you should return it to the
   store and get a refund.

**2 Choose the correct word to complete the
sentences.**

1 I never buy designer clothes. *On/In* fact, I often buy
   used clothes.
2 If you're worried about what to wear don't worry; help
   is *by/at* hand from our fashion designer.
3 Mini skirts went *past/out* of fashion years ago.
4 Charles is involved *in/at* designing theatre costumes.
5 My friend has a pair of trainers with a logo *at/on*
   them.
6 I admire Sandra *for/by* her fashion sense.

**3 Complete the sentences with the correct form of
the words in capitals.**

1 The clothes Sue wears are really
   ....original........ .   ORIGIN
2 Ties aren't very ....   FASHION
   these days.
3 I wanted a pair of combat trousers and
   ...., the shop had   FORTUNATE
   one pair left.
4 She has a detailed ....   KNOW
   of fashion.
5 I'd like to be a fashion
   ....   DESIGN
6 Can I have a new pair of
   .... to wear?   TRAIN
7 They're running a good
   .... campaign.   ADVERTISE

Reading

**1 Read the text and choose the sentence (A–H) that
best fits each gap (1–7). There is one extra
sentence which you do not need to use.**

A Organic cotton jeans are now 'cool', and so are shoes
  made from recycled materials.
B It was plastic, and was virtually identical to the type
  of plastic carrier bag they'd give you in a supermarket.
C Without brand names, goods cost a great deal less,
  which is good news for less wealthy fashion hunters.
D So if you thought they were all individually produced,
  think again!
E And fashion prices go up every year, which makes it
  very hard to keep up – unless you're rich and famous,
  of course.
F Without a famous logo, the products would be
  practically worthless.
G That's why celebrities want brand products, as well as
  fashion-conscious teenagers.
H These imitation goods are illegal, of course, but some
  bargain-hunters are quite happy to buy them.

Ethical Fashion?

Nowadays, if you've got plenty of cash, it's trendy to buy goods with designer labels. Having sunglasses with a famous logo, or designer jeans, is supposed to be 'cool' and make other people look up to you. 1) ..6.. When they go out looking for a bag or a jacket, it's the brand name these shoppers care about, rather than the quality of the goods. As a result, many fashion companies are more concerned about displaying their brand name than ensuring goods are well made. And there's another problem with designer products. They're fantastically expensive! 2) ..... Fashion houses realise this. That's why they've started bringing out more affordable versions of the major labels called 'diffusion brands'. You can find these cheaper brands everywhere – in airport shops and holiday resorts, or even in markets. They include cheaply produced sunglasses, perfumes, belts and key rings.

3) ..... But with it, they become a 'must-have' for people who want to show off.

So what are people really getting when they buy brand-name goods? Originally, companies used labels on their products to indicate they were of top quality, and to indicate where they were made. But these days, brand name goods, especially diffusion brands, are often mass-produced in factories in the Far East.

4) .....

Sometimes shoppers are offered fake designer goods instead of the genuine articles. 5) ..... It's a false economy because the products are often poorly made and soon fall to pieces. The question is, are diffusion brand products very much better?

The rush to buy designer brands has created a mad, mad world. Nowadays, two products may be sold at hugely different prices just because one has a brand name. A famous company recently brought out a bag with a brand name on the front. 6) ..... But with the brand name attached, it became a 'must have' item and cost hundreds of dollars.

If you think the designer label scene has gone too far, you may be pleased to hear about a new trend. It's becoming 'cool' to think about the social and environmental impacts of fashion and to shop in an ethical way. Ethical fashion companies make clothes from natural, chemical-free, sustainable materials. 7) ..... There are designer labels on these too, but the products come first. If this trend continues, we can be 'cool' and stylish, *and* help the world at the same time.

Shopping

→ For exercises 1–6 see pages 98 and 102 in your Students' Book.

1 Complete the sentences with the correct nouns.

label   market   name   store   symbol   ~~victim~~

1 She's a *fashion* .... victim .... – she buys the latest clothes even if they look awful on her.
2 If you can't find what you want in the local boutique, try the *department* .... in the High Street.
3 Celebrities sometimes buy themselves a Rolls Royce as a *status* ....
4 Ferrari is an internationally famous *brand* ....
5 If you want jeans with a *designer* .... they'll cost a lot more than usual.
6 If you want to buy a car produced on the *mass* .... you could try a make like Ford or Fiat.

2 Choose the correct preposition to complete the sentences.

1 My brother's going to drive round the block to show *off/out* his new car.
2 Fashions change so fast it's hard to keep *on/up* with them.
3 The clothes I bought last year are really *beyond/out of* fashion now.
4 Designer labels are popular *between/among* young people in many countries.
5 Three-quarter-length shorts were trendy last year but I think they're on their way *out/off* now.

3 Complete the sentences with the correct adjectives.

~~exclusive~~   flattering   sophisticated   stereotyped   trendy

1 That boutique is extremely ...... exclusive ......; their clothes cost a fortune.
2 Those sunglasses are the wrong shape for you – they don't look very ....
3 Ethical fashion is becoming quite .... but it might go out of fashion soon.
4 Teenagers are often .... as moody and rebellious.
5 For the cocktail party, my sister wore a traditional little black dress and she looked really ....

4 Complete the sentences with the correct form of the words in capitals.

1 The shop assistant was very ..... persuasive ...... but didn't manage to sell us anything.   PERSUADE
2 I saw a really funny .... on TV yesterday.   ADVERTISE
3 The interior of a Rolls Royce is extremely ....   LUXURY
4 Amanda has a really .... smile.   APPEAL
5 There's a lot of .... between designers to get shops to buy their clothes.   COMPETE
6 They've reduced the price of their jeans as part of a winter sales ....   PROMOTE

5 Match the words (1–5) to the words (a–e) to make compound nouns.

1 chain   a promotion
2 shop   b room
3 advertising   c shopping
4 window   d store
5 fitting   e assistant

6 Choose the correct phrasal verbs to complete the sentences.

1 Shall I ask the assistant if I can go to the fitting room to . B . these jeans?
   A put on   **B** try on
2 Tina's only having a party because she wants to ..... her engagement ring.
   A show off   **B** show up

3 You're walking too fast – I can't ..... with you!
   A keep in   **B** keep up
4 I should ..... your coat or you'll get too hot.
   A take out   **B** take off
5 The zip's stuck so I can't ..... my jeans.
   A do up   **B** do in
6 I'm hoping to ..... a bargain at the sales.
   A pick off   **B** pick up
7 John's shoes tend to ..... very quickly because he does a lot of running.
   A wear out   **B** wear off
8 If you want to buy designer sunglasses you'll have to ..... for ages!
   A save in   **B** save up

Reported speech and reporting verbs

➜ For exercises 1–5 see pages 99 and 103 in your Students' Book.

1 **Choose the correct form to complete the sentences.**

1 My friend asked *that I go/me to go* shopping with her.
2 The store manager said the thief *has stolen/had stolen* three cameras.
3 My brother *said/told* me he was sick of shopping.
4 The customer inquired *whether the sale had begun/the sale had begun.*
5 Nobody told me the store *closed/had closed.*
6 Dad warned me *to not spend/not to spend* too much money.

2 **Rewrite the sentences using the words in capitals. Use between two and five words, including the word given.**

1 'It is a bargain, Tom.'
  TOLD
  Tom's mother .....told him it was..... a bargain.
2 'When does the shop shut, please?'
  KNOW
  The customer wanted to .... shut.
3 'Can I try the jeans on, please?'
  ASKED
  I .... the jeans on.
4 'How do I close this bag?'
  TO
  I asked the shop assistant how ....
5 'We've spent our money.'
  SAID
  My friends .... money.
6 'Don't touch anything!'
  ME
  Mum .... anything.
7 'I forgot to buy a card!' said Nadia.
  REALISED
  Nadia .... to buy a card.
8 'Do you need a receipt?'
  INQUIRED
  The shop assistant .... a receipt.

3 **Choose the word or phrase that best completes the sentence.**

1 The store detective accused him ..A...
  A of stealing   **B** to steal
2 My friends advised ..... it.
  A that I bought   **B** me to buy
3 John apologised ..... the glass.
  A to break   **B** for breaking
4 You promised ..... me a present.
  A to buy   **B** buying
5 Jessica insisted ..... for lunch.
  A on paying   **B** to pay
6 They warned us ..... our bags on the counter.
  A to not leave   **B** not to leave
7 She offered ..... me a refund.
  A to give   **B** giving
8 Mum encouraged ..... a new phone.
  A that I bought   **B** me to buy

4 **Complete the sentences with the correct form of the verbs in brackets.**

1 Anna denied ....breaking....... (break) the glass.
2 The manager told us .... (not/touch) the goods.
3 My friend reminded me .... (buy) a birthday card.
4 The man admitted .... (steal) the radio.
5 Terrorists threatened .... (blow up) the store.

5 **Complete the text with the correct form of the verbs in brackets.**

Last week, my friend Sonya invited me 1) ....to go........ (go) window shopping with her. I agreed. I suggested 2) .... (take) a bus into the city centre because I'd heard a big new department store was opening in town and I wanted 3) .... (check) it out. It was a good idea because Sonya loved the fashions. I persuaded her 4) .... (try on) the most amazing futuristic dress. It can change colour according to your mood! Unfortunately, the sales assistant guessed we couldn't afford to buy it and accused us of 5) .... (waste) her time, so we had to leave. There was a car showroom next to the store and I insisted on 6) .... (have) a look round. I love cars! They had the most amazing underwater car on show. The salesman offered 7) .... (show) us how it worked. What a great idea! But Sonya threatened 8) .... (leave) without me if I didn't hurry. So I apologised to the salesman for 9) .... (have to) rush off. He told me 10) .... (not/worry) and said I could go back and have a good look at the car another time!

Use your English

1 Read the text and choose the best answer, A, B, C or D.

BRANDING

Companies started branding products 1) ..B.. in the 1800s. There were very 2) ..... laws to regulate manufacturing in those days so there were plenty of dangerous products 3) ..... sale, including fake medicines! Reputable companies 4) ..... started branding their own goods to show they were safe and of good quality. In order to 5) ..... these brands successfully, the companies turned to advertising. They discovered that good advertising can influence sales in 6) ..... big way. Of course commercial advertising is big business 7) .... And it is everywhere! 8) ..... on the TV, or go to the movies, and you'll see ads for nearly everything. Sometimes you don't even realise a product is 9) ..... advertised. In the movie *Minority Report*, the character played by Tom Cruise owns a phone on 10) ..... the *Nokia* logo is clearly displayed, 11) ..... his watch is engraved with the *Bulgari* logo, so you have no doubt about the make. Similarly, in the Bond film *Casino Royale*, the vehicles James Bond drives and the gadgets he uses have clear brand 12) .... Hidden advertising 13) ..... this is very effective.

1	**A** long	**B** back	**C** far	**D** way
2	**A** a few	**B** a lot	**C** few	**D** lots
3	**A** on	**B** in	**C** at	**D** by
4	**A** so	**B** however	**C** although	**D** therefore
5	**A** show	**B** compete	**C** market	**D** appeal
6	**A** the	**B** a	**C** this	**D** some
7	**A** nowadays	**B** presently	**C** recently	**D** lately
8	**A** Press	**B** Log	**C** Push	**D** Switch
9	**A** having	**B** getting	**C** being	**D** making
10	**A** that	**B** which	**C** whom	**D** where
11	**A** and	**B** but	**C** also	**D** except
12	**A** titles	**B** signs	**C** names	**D** signatures
13	**A** same	**B** alike	**C** as	**D** like

2 Complete the text with <u>one</u> word which best fits each gap.

Last week I went 1) ....on.......... the worst shopping trip of my life. My sister Alice had asked me 2) .... I'd help her buy a new dress. It wasn't my idea of fun but I agreed 3) .... go. She promised that it 4) .... not take long and suggested 5) .... to see my favourite film in the afternoon. She promised 6) .... could go for a meal afterwards, too. But the trip turned into a nightmare! Alice insisted 7) .... visiting every shop in the High Street. She 8) .... on dresses in every possible size and colour, but she didn't like any of them. Lunchtime came but Alice 9) .... me there was no time to eat. When I begged 10) .... to make her mind up, she lost her temper and accused me 11) .... ruining her day. By the end of the day, she hadn't found anything she liked and we went home. She never apologised 12) .... making us miss the film. And I never got my meal. It's 13) .... last time I go shopping with Alice, that's for sure!

Writing *an email*

➔ For exercises 1–6 see pages 104–105 in your Students' Book.

1 **Read the writing task below and answer the questions.**

1 Who is going to read your email?

2 Will your reader expect you to use a formal style, or an informal, chatty style?

You have received this email from a penfriend in the UK and made a few notes about it. Write an email back to your penfriend in 120–150 words, using all your notes.

ask about what he'd prefer

give details

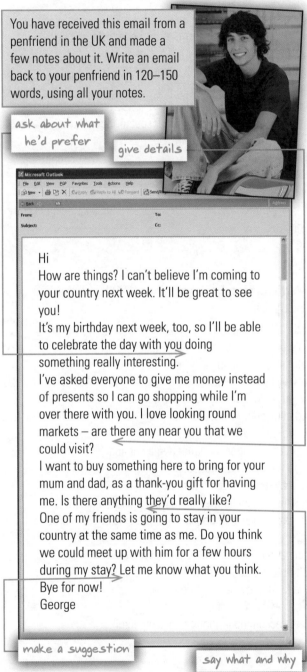

Microsoft Outlook

File Edit View PGP Favorites Tools Actions Help

New ▾ | ⏷ ✉ ✕ | Reply Reply to All Forward | Send/Re...

Back

From: To:

Subject: Cc:

Hi

How are things? I can't believe I'm coming to your country next week. It'll be great to see you!

It's my birthday next week, too, so I'll be able to celebrate the day with you doing something really interesting.

I've asked everyone to give me money instead of presents so I can go shopping while I'm over there with you. I love looking round markets – are there any near you that we could visit?

I want to buy something here to bring for your mum and dad, as a thank-you gift for having me. Is there anything they'd really like?

One of my friends is going to stay in your country at the same time as me. Do you think we could meet up with him for a few hours during my stay? Let me know what you think.

Bye for now!

George

make a suggestion

say what and why

2 **What must you say in your email? Complete this list of points.**

1 Ask what ....

2 Describe what kind ....

3 ....
....
....

3 **Answer these questions to get ideas for what to put in your email.**

1 What question can you ask George to find out his preferences for his birthday? Think of two different suggestions you could make for what to do for the day.

2 Are there any markets in or near your town? What are they like? What kind of things do they sell? Are they worth visiting? Why/Why not?

3 What present do you think your mum and dad would like from the UK? Why would they like it?

4 Do you want to arrange for you, George and his friend to meet up? Why/Why not? Where could you meet and what could you all do?

4 **Put these phrases into the correct column.**

Would you like to …
You asked about …
Do you fancy …ing?
Regarding your suggestion about …
We could …
Turning to your question about …
I suggest that we …
Now, about …

Asking about preferences/Making suggestions	Referring to a new topic

5 **Here is a possible paragraph plan for your email. Decide which ideas to include in each paragraph and note them down.**

Paragraph 1 (Introduction) Opening remarks
Paragraph 2 ....
Paragraph 3 ....
Paragraph 4 ....
Paragraph 5 ....
Paragraph 6 (Conclusion) Closing remarks

6 **Now write your answer to the writing task in Exercise 1.**

Do you need more practice?

Go to: CD-ROM, Unit 9.

10 Breaking the rules

Vocabulary

→ For exercises 1–3 see pages 106–107 in your Students' Book.

1 **Complete the sentences with the correct form of the words in capitals.**

1 The police were worried that the chemicals were dangerous but they turned out to be completely ......harmless....... HARM
2 When Tom was a teenager he was very .... REBEL
3 Watching the police dogs at work was quite .... EXCITE
4 Someone was caught trying to .... the factory. VANDAL
5 She claimed to be innocent but she was clearly .... GUILT
6 The judge decided to .... the robbers. PRISON
7 He pretended to be shopping but in .... he was stealing clothes from the store. REAL
8 As ...., they had to clean the graffiti off the walls. PUNISH
9 The police .... caught up with the criminals. EVENTUAL
10 The .... on the cheque turned out to be a forgery. SIGN

2 **Choose the correct words to complete the sentences.**

1 The detective is good *in/at* his job.
2 Terry is *on/in* trouble with the police.
3 Don't walk through the forest *by/on* your own after dark.
4 One of the gang suggested robbing a bank and the others went *on/along* with the idea.
5 Don't make excuses. You shouldn't have been driving so fast *in/on* the first place.
6 Don't get involved *in/at* crime or you'll regret it.
7 When someone picked my pocket I had no idea *of/at* all.
8 Many burglaries take place *in/at* night.
9 I know you want to catch the thief so what plan have you got *on/in* mind?
10 My neighbour turned *off/out* to be a bank robber!

3 **Complete the sentences with these verbs.**

learn   go   rob   play   ~~break~~   get   pass   change

1 After a while, detectives managed to .... break .... the code and catch the spy.
2 The judge said he hoped the teenager would .... a lesson after the punishment he was given.
3 Criminals often think they will never .... caught.
4 The threat of prison made him .... his ways.
5 Before Dad could become a police inspector he had to .... an exam.
6 The gang persuaded Jane to .... shoplifting.
7 It's not a crime to .... truant but it's not very clever, either.
8 Somebody tried to .... a bank in the city centre last night.

Reading

1 **Read the article. Match the questions (1–16) with the detectives (A–D).**

Which of the detectives
1 lives in a university town. ..A.
2 is a practising musician. .....
3 has previously been married. .....
4 takes a great deal of care with his clothes. .....
5 has had an academic education. .....
6 detests being in an office. .....
7 shows great courage when meeting a criminal. .....
8 arrived in the UK as a refugee. .....
9 has a hobby that links with his job. .....
10 changes his physical appearance from time to time. .....
11 doesn't have much confidence in people who are in charge of things. .....
12 sometimes falls in love with women who break the law. .....
13 is respected and admired by his colleagues. .....
14 makes a lot of inquiries that don't seem important. .....
15 doesn't show his feelings in public. .....
16 shares his accommodation with a companion. .....

Detectives in fiction

Sandra West gives us details about four great fictional detectives

A Chief Inspector **Morse** features in a series of crime novels created by writer Colin Dexter. Morse works in Oxford, home of the famous university. He is supposed to have attended the university himself, but a broken romance caused him to fail his exams and he had to leave. Morse drives a vintage car and loves beer and opera. A single man, he finds romance a number of times but these romantic episodes always end in failure. Either the women turn out to be criminals, or they get fed up with taking second place to his police work. He's a very likeable character, being sensitive and caring towards those in trouble. However, he can also be moody and bad-tempered. He's brainy and has a wide knowledge of the world, which is why he's so good at his favourite free-time activity – doing crossword puzzles. He uses the same approach to solving these as he does to solving a crime.

B Chief Inspector **John Rebus** features in a series of crime novels written by Ian Rankin. Rebus works in the capital of Scotland, Edinburgh, a city the writer paints as dark and mysterious. Rebus, like his city, keeps his emotions hidden from the people around him. He's a complex man – hard and obstinate on the outside, but generous and kind at heart. A good detective, he hates desk work and is happiest when out on the street solving crimes. He identifies with people who are down on their luck, and distrusts those who are in authority over others. Rebus loves books and rock music. He likes women, too. Divorced from his wife, he has a string of romantic relationships, but none last very long.

C **Hercule Poirot** is a brilliant Belgian detective who features in the novels of Agatha Christie. A retired police officer, Poirot is supposed to have worked as a private detective in Europe before escaping to England during wartime. He's a rather eccentric little man, who dresses incredibly elegantly, and has a stiff military moustache. He is curious and perceptive and he has a remarkable brain which he refers to as his 'little grey cells'. Poirot uses psychology to solve a series of complex crimes. He asks a lot of apparently pointless questions, notes down revealing remarks from his suspects and notices the tiniest of details. Other policemen make fun of his eccentric ways, but Poirot always comes out on top. Most cases end with a dramatic scene where Poirot names the murderer and explains how he solved the crime. This scene confirms that he is 'the greatest mind in Europe'.

D **Sherlock Holmes** features in the novels of Sir Arthur Conan Doyle and is possibly the most famous fictional private detective ever created. Holmes lives in London, at 221B Baker Street, with his friend and assistant Doctor Watson. Holmes appears cold, superior and arrogant, but he is capable of warmth and friendship. He uses scientific means to solve his cases. It's by finding clues – the type of soil on a shoe, a dropped cigarette, a fingerprint, that he can build up a picture of what has happened and then identify the criminal responsible. He's quite fearless, often confronting violent murderers alone. Holmes is single and has no long-term romantic relationships. He plays the violin well, and is good at boxing and swordplay. He sometimes wears disguises so even his friends don't recognise him. He prepares dramatic traps to capture criminals. Only then does he explain what made him suspect them. His methods always impress the local policemen around him because they are far more efficient and effective than anyone else's.

Crime

➜ For exercises 1–7 see pages 108 and 112 in your Students' Book.

1 Choose the correct word to complete the sentences.

1 The girl was found *innocent/ guilty* so the judge set her free.
2 Criminals think they're clever but they usually end up in *trial/ court*.
3 The tramp was *assassinated/ murdered* in the park.
4 She saw the men put a bomb in the car so she was an important *victim/witness*.
5 The shoplifter was *sentenced/ charged* to two months' imprisonment.
6 A gang of youths *attacked/ vandalised* a man in the street.

2 Match the verbs (1–6) with the nouns (a–f).

1 catch   a a bank
2 commit   b a decision
3 rob   c a fine
4 steal   d a criminal
5 pay   e a watch
6 make   f a crime

3 Complete the sentences with a suitable preposition.

1 He was charged .... **with** .... shoplifting.
2 The terrorist will be put .... trial next week.
3 The police arrested the boys .... vandalising the building.
4 Goods were stolen .... the store.
5 She was found guilty .... shoplifting.
6 The barrister was responsible .... defending the suspect in court.

4 Complete the sentences with the correct nouns.

ringleader   gang   conviction   ~~lawyer~~   case   jury   evidence   court

1 When I leave school I want to study to be a .... **lawyer** ....
2 All twelve members of the .... found the man guilty.
3 The youths went round in a .... and got into mischief.
4 She had a .... on her records for drunken driving, so she couldn't join the police force.
5 The police had to release the suspect because they didn't have enough .... to prove his guilt.
6 John was the .... of the group so it was he who gave the orders.
7 Detectives are investigating a .... of attempted robbery.
8 He's been charged, and he goes to .... next week.

5 Complete the table.

Crime	Verb	Person
1 shoplifting		a
2	to forge	a
3 mugging		a mugger
4	to burgle	
5		a robber
6 theft		
7	to murder	
8	to defraud	a fraudster
9 vandalism		a vandal
10 assault		an assailant

6 Choose the word or phrase that best completes the sentence.

1 Instead of sending the thief to prison, the judge .**B**. with a warning.
   A put him off   B let him off
2 Don't think you'll ..... what you've done!
   A get away with   B go down with
3 Robbers ..... paintings worth millions of dollars.
   A took away with   B made off with
4 The terrorists ..... the attack because they realised the police were watching them.
   A called off   B brought down
5 When their parents were away, the youths ..... a great deal of mischief.
   A did away with   B got up to

7 Complete the sentences with the correct form of these verbs.

forge   mug   murder   ~~shoplift~~   trick   vandalise

1 Store detectives caught the woman ...... **shoplifting** ...... in the clothes department.
2 Three boys .... the old man as he was walking through the alley.
3 She .... her mother's signature on a cheque and tried to cash it.
4 Stop those boys! They're .... the swings in the playground.
5 The gunmen .... another of their gang and tried to hide the body.
6 A pick-pocket .... me into looking the other way and then stole my wallet.

Wishes and regrets

→ For exercises 1–2 see page 109 in your Students' Book.

1 Choose the correct words to complete the sentences.

1 I wish Paul *won't/wouldn't* play truant any more.
2 She wishes she *hadn't joined/didn't join* the gang.
3 They regret *to break/breaking* the law.
4 We *shouldn't have written/shouldn't write* graffiti on those walls yesterday.
5 I wish I *would be/were* a lawyer.
6 I wish I *could/would* stop my brother getting into trouble.

2 Complete the sentences with the correct form of the verbs in brackets.

1 I wish I .... *knew* .... (know) the answer to the problem!
2 Catherine wishes she .... (not steal) from the shop.
3 If only Peter .... (leave) the gang he hangs round with! They'll get him into big trouble one day.
4 Tessa regrets .... (tell) so many lies.
5 The jury wished they .... (have) more evidence to go on.

Linking words and structures

→ For exercises 3–4 see page 113 in your Students' Book.

3 Choose the word or phrase that best completes the sentence.

1 He was ..B.. scared he ran away.
   A such   **B** so
2 The robber wore large sunglasses ..... hide his appearance.
   A in order to   **B** in order that
3 Lock the door ..... someone tries to break in.
   A because of   **B** in case
4 The police couldn't catch the criminals ..... all their efforts.
   A despite   **B** although
5 ..... the judge was kind-hearted, he was also very fair.
   A However   **B** While
6 They put CCTV cameras in the store ..... catch any shoplifters.
   A so as to   **B** so that

4 Complete the text with <u>one</u> word which best fits each gap.

STOP THIEF!

Have you ever wished you 1) .... *could* .... spend a day as a Roman centurion? Steve Jordan joined a Historical Society in 2) .... to do just that. Members of the Society dress up as Romans 3) .... that they can bring history alive. They put on displays in schools, museums, parks 4) .... other open areas. Audiences learn a lot about life in the Roman Empire due 5) .... their efforts. Last week Steve and his companions travelled to the ancient Roman city of York so 6) .... to take part in a big festival. They put on a mock battle, dressed as soldiers from a Roman legion. But they got very tired because 7) .... the heat, so they took a break. They 8) .... having a chat, when they noticed that some men 9) .... climbed onto the roof of a nearby building. 'I don't think those guys should 10) .... climbed up there!' Steve said. 'I bet they're up to no good!' He was right. The men were stealing valuable metal off the roof! 'Come on,' he shouted, and he and his companions, still in Roman costume, ran to catch 11) .... thieves. But the thieves saw them coming and 12) .... a result, they managed to escape. They got 13) .... a fright, however, that they left all the valuable metal behind!

Use your English

1 Complete the text with the correct form of the words in brackets.

Protect your identity!

It may seem 1) .... *amazing* .... (amaze), but all sorts of people want to steal your identity. 2) .... (crime) can get hold of your personal details in a 3) .... (vary) of ways. Papers containing important 4) .... (inform) are often stolen from rubbish bins. Or plastic cards can be taken and 5) .... (copy) by dishonest waiters or shop assistants. The following 6) .... (advise) will help you to protect your identity.

- Don't leave 7) .... (value) items like plastic cards lying around where anyone can see them.
- Be very 8) .... (care) with official papers and documents, and destroy them when you've finished with them.
- If you give personal details over the phone or internet, make 9) .... (extreme) sure that other people can't see or hear you.
- Be certain that nobody can read your mail without your 10) .... (know).
- And finally, if you are 11) .... (worry) that you might have lost your mobile phone or plastic cards, tell someone immediately.

2 Rewrite the sentences using the words in capitals. Use between two and five words, including the word given.

1 I'm sorry I told you a lie.
NOT
I regret ...... *not telling* ...... you the truth.

2 We were afraid the alarm might ring too loudly so we didn't open the door.
CASE
We didn't open the door .... too loudly.

3 They put photographs in the paper so that they could catch the criminal.
ORDER
They put photographs in the paper .... the criminal.

4 It was wrong of you to steal the watch.
HAVE
You .... the watch.

5 The painting was so valuable that nobody would insure it.
SUCH
It was .... nobody would insure it.

6 Despite his great strength, he couldn't fight off his attacker.
VERY
Although .... he couldn't fight off his attacker .

7 'I'd like to be a police officer, not a car mechanic,' John sighed.
WISHED
John .... instead of a car mechanic.

8 I'm sorry I didn't report the theft to the police.
ONLY
If .... the theft to the police!

Writing *an essay*

➔ For exercises 1–8 see pages 114–115 in your Students' Book.

1 **Read the writing task and answer the questions.**

> Some people blame working mothers for an increase in teenage crime. Do you agree? Write an essay in 120–180 words.

Which of these questions must you write about in your essay? Tick the correct option.
1 Are more young people committing crimes these days?
2 Are children of working mothers more likely to get into trouble and commit crimes?

2 **Read statements A and B, and the lists of reasons. Then add at least one more reason to each list.**

A *It is <u>good</u> for a child to have a working mother because*
  – her job makes life more interesting for her, and for her children
  – she keeps up with modern ideas and technology and can help her kids with this
  – she hasn't got enough time to nag her kids about unimportant things
  – it teaches her kids to be independent and responsible
  – she can afford to pay for visits to the cinema and other treats

B *It is <u>bad</u> for a child to have a working mother because*
  – she may be too exhausted to help with homework
  – she may be in a bad mood all the time because she is stressed out at work
  – she may be too tired to talk to her kids in the evenings

3 **Decide which statement, A or B, you agree with.**

4 **Match the linking words (1–8) to their use (a–h).**

1 In fact,
2 As a result,
3 In order to
4 All in all,
5 For instance,
6 Because
7 On the other hand,
8 What's more,

a to show result
b before a reason
c to add more points in an argument
d to contrast a positive with a negative idea
e to introduce an example
f to show purpose
g to emphasise a point
h to round off the end of an essay

5 **Complete the gaps in these sentences with linking words from Exercise 4.**

1 Some young people may go wrong if there's nobody home to supervise them. *On the other hand*, it may bring out a sense of independence in others.
2 Working mothers can sometimes make their children's lives better. ...., the money they earn may pay for their kids to go to drama class or have sports tuition.
3 Some women have to work .... pay the bills. It doesn't mean their children will become criminals!
4 Children of working mothers are not disadvantaged. ...., they are often better off than other children.
5 Children whose mothers work are often more responsible than other kids. ...., they're often more independent, too.

6 **Write the following sections of an essay in the correct place on the paragraph plan below:**
  – a summary/restatement of my opinions
  – what people with an opposite view to me think, and why. Why I still think my views outweigh theirs
  – introductory statements
  – reasons why I think children with working mothers are/are not likely to get involved in crime

Paragraph 1 ....
Paragraph 2 ....
Paragraph 3 ....
Paragraph 4 ....

7 **Look back to Exercise 2 and choose the best three reasons to support your opinion. Then choose one or two reasons for the opposite view to yours.**

8 **Now write your answer to the writing task in Exercise 1. Remember to explain your reasons and give examples where appropriate.**

Do you need more practice?
Go to: CD-ROM, Unit 10.

69

Grammar

1 **Choose the correct word or words to complete the sentences.**

1 I took an umbrella with me in *order/case* it rained.
2 Dad congratulated me *in/on* passing my driving test.
3 He committed such *a/so* terrible crime he was sent to gaol for life.
4 *While/However* not approving of the man's actions, the judge didn't believe they were illegal.
5 He *refused/denied* breaking into the bank.
6 I wish I *would/could* join the police force but my dad wants me to take over his business instead.
7 I regret *breaking/to break* the law.
8 The police officer *said/told* me to report to the police station tomorrow morning.

2 **Rewrite the sentences using the words in capitals. Use between two and five words, including the word given.**

1 'Can I have a refund?' he asked.
WHETHER
He asked whether he could have a refund.
2 My sister regrets buying those boots.
WISHES
My sister .... those boots.
3 'Let's have a coffee,' Lucy said.
SUGGESTED
Lucy .... a coffee.
4 'I'm sorry I broke the zip,' John said.
APOLOGISED
John .... the zip.
5 The shop assistant said I had stolen the camera.
ACCUSED
The shop assistant .... the camera.
6 It was wrong of you to tell a lie.
SHOULD
You .... a lie.
7 I haven't got enough money for a ring.
AFFORD
I wish .... a ring.
8 'Don't leave your wallet lying around,' the police officer said.
WARNED
The police officer .... my wallet lying around.

3 **Choose the word or phrase that best completes the sentence.**

1 The judge insisted .B. for what we'd done.
   A us to apologise
   B that we apologise
   C us apologising
   D for us to apologise
2 She advised ..... home.
   A that we go
   B us to go
   C us going
   D we go
3 The terrorist threatened ..... the hostages.
   A shooting
   B shot
   C he shoot
   D to shoot
4 If only those boys ..... bullying me!
   A would stop
   B stopped
   C will stop
   D stopping
5 He withdrew money from the bank ..... to buy a new computer.
   A so
   B in order
   C due
   D since
6 It was ..... awful weather we put off our shopping trip for another day.
   A such a
   B so
   C such
   D a such

Vocabulary

4 **Complete the sentences with <u>one</u> word which best fits each gap.**

1 Harrods is a famous department ....store......... in London that sells all kinds of things from cookers to silk pyjamas.
2 Clothes made for the mass .... are always cheaper than individually made items.
3 Mum hadn't got enough cash to pay for the sweater so she bought it with her credit ....
4 Why don't you go and try that suit on in the fitting ....?
5 The shoplifter was stopped by a store .... who saw her take the watch.
6 Just because we're broke, it doesn't mean we can't go window- ....
7 Rich people like to be seen driving Jaguars because they are a status ....
8 Designer trainers are a real must-......................... item for trendy teenagers at the moment.

5 **Complete the sentences with the correct form of the words in capitals.**

1 Sorry! I ...misunderstood... your instructions. UNDERSTAND
2 The spy was sent for .... and will appear in court next month. TRY
3 He was caught attempting to .... the bank and was sent to prison. FRAUD
4 It was .... of her to take books and pens from the bookstore without paying. HONEST
5 If you .... the teacher, you'll get into trouble! OBEY
6 At the London Dungeon you can see waxworks of some of the most .... murderers and villains in English history. FAMOUS
7 You shouldn't .... your parents. RESPECT
8 The judge made him clean up the graffiti as a .... PUNISH

6 **Choose the correct word or words to complete the sentences.**

1 Dan has been *arrested*/*charged* for spraying graffiti in the town centre.
2 I want to look cool but some fashions don't *appeal*/*respect* to me at all!
3 He was guilty but the police let him *out*/*off* because he was so young.
4 Tracksuits used to be trendy but they're a bit *behind*/*out of* fashion these days.
5 Bags, belts and jewellery are called fashion *accessories*/*bargains*.
6 I saw what happened in the accident so the police asked me to act as a *defendant*/*witness*.
7 If you *commit*/*perform* a crime, you could end up in prison.
8 Many teenagers feel that there should be *sterner*/*stricter* punishment for crime.

7 **Choose the word or phrase that best completes the sentence.**

1 I wish Adam didn't have such a high opinion of himself. He's showing .B. again.
   A up
   B off
   C on
   D out
2 Fashions change so quickly it's sometimes hard to ..... up with them!
   A put
   B do
   C make
   D keep
3 Tom has started shoplifting but he won't get away ..... it for long. Somebody will catch him one of these days.
   A with
   B from
   C by
   D for
4 Robbers broke into the safe and ..... with the jewellery.
   A got out
   B went away
   C made off
   D took out
5 My brother and his friends are always ..... to mischief.
   A going off
   B breaking in
   C coming off
   D getting up
6 Quick! Get hold ..... the dog or he'll run away!
   A on
   B of
   C with
   D for

11 A tall story

Vocabulary

➜ For exercises 1–3 see pages 118–119 in your Students' Book.

1 Complete the sentences with the correct form of these verbs.

~~gasp~~   survive   disturb   wonder   inscribe   ignore
spread   gather   peer   threaten

1 Onlookers .... *gasped* .... out loud when they caught sight of the magnificent tomb.
2 The archaeologist .... through a tiny hole, into the dark chamber.
3 Ancient grave builders had .... a curse on the side of the tomb.
4 The curse .... anyone who entered the tomb with death.
5 When the chief archaeologist died, people .... whether the mummy's curse had fallen on him.
6 Carnarvon died shortly after entering the tomb but Carter .... for many years afterwards.
7 News that a new tomb had been discovered .... quickly.
8 Anyone who .... the sanctity of a pharaoh's tomb risks being cursed.
9 Many people .... together around the tomb to watch Carter open it.
10 By .... the curse and entering the tomb, Carter and his companions were inviting danger.

2 Choose the correct preposition to complete the sentences.

1 They ignored the danger *at/in* their peril!
2 Everyone stared *in/on* wonder when they saw the treasures.
3 *At/In* time, all of the pharaohs' tombs were discovered.
4 Tutankhamen's body was surrounded *from/with* precious objects.
5 Carter thought his discovery would make him happy but *in/on* fact it did the opposite.

3 Complete the sentence with a suitable word. The first letter has been given.

1 The boy king had a .... *wound* .... on his cheek, maybe from a knife cut.
2 The ancient Egyptians believed that the s......................... goes on living after the body dies.
3 He became king when he was a boy and his r......................... lasted for just a few years.
4 Tutankhamen may have been murdered by some of his e......................... at court.
5 Carter's servants thought his pet canary was a lucky c......................... .
6 After working for so long on the excavation, Carter was completely e......................... .

Reading

1 Read the article and choose the best answer, A, B, C or D.

1 Who does 'they' refer to in line 3 of the text?
   A the authorities   B the villagers
   C the creatures   D the scientists
2 In paragraph 2, the writer suggests that witnesses who describe the height of the creatures may be
   A telling the truth.   B making a mistake.
   C exaggerating the facts. D telling a lie.
3 Who does 'it' refer to in line 10, paragraph 3?
   A the creature   B the photo
   C the experience   D the wood
4 Why were some scientists convinced that the creature in the photograph was not human?
   A Its feet were bigger than human feet.
   B Its footprints were too large.
   C It took longer steps than humans.
   D Its prints were not a human shape.
5 According to the writer, the suggestion that a species of animal is living among us, unnoticed, is
   A improbable.   B ridiculous.
   C possible.   D unlikely.
6 It appears that Native Americans regard creatures like the Bigfoot as
   A a useful food source.   B a danger to hunters.
   C friends to humans.   D intelligent enemies.
7 What do scientists need to find in order to prove that the Bigfoot exist?
   A monkeys   B records
   C apes   D bones
8 What does 'reclusive' mean in the final paragraph?
   A aggressive   B friendly
   C unsociable   D harmless

Jungle mystery

Sightings of mysterious animals have been reported from many remote regions of our world. But are they fact or fantasy? Steve Brown looks into the subject.

Terrified villagers in India have recently reported seeing huge human-like creatures roaming the jungle. They call them 'Mande Burung', or 'Jungle Men'. The authorities, mystified by the reports, are considering a number of possibilities. Firstly, the villagers may have mistaken a common animal for something else (at a distance, identifying animals can be difficult). Secondly, they could all be lying. If neither of these explanations is true, there remains one more, amazing possibility. A species unknown to scientists but very like ourselves is wandering this planet, virtually undetected!

Of course, people in remote regions of the world have been claiming this for years. Sightings of giant, man-like creatures have frequently been reported from places as far apart as the Far East, Africa, Australia and Europe. The 'monsters' are called 'Sasquatch' or 'Bigfoot' in the USA; in Asia they're known as 'Yeti'; in Africa 'Kikomba'. The descriptions given in all these places are remarkably similar. The creatures are said to be tall and powerful, and covered in dark brown or red hair. However, some witnesses claim the beasts are about 10 foot tall, while others say they're shorter. This variation is not necessarily a problem given that some of the creatures might have been juveniles and thus not fully grown.

Two Americans claimed to have seen and photographed a Bigfoot some years ago. They were travelling through a thick wood when they saw a huge, hairy creature walking on two feet. They ran towards it but it vanished into the trees. They said they were afraid to follow it into the wood in case it turned and attacked them. But when they described their experience and published a photograph of the creature, many experts dismissed it as a hoax. They said it was the image of a man dressed in a monkey suit.

However, the photos did convince a few well known and reputable scientists. Having measured the distance between each footprint, they concluded that the creature's stride was much longer than that of any human. They suggested it could be a member of an ape-like species that originally lived in Asia. The jawbones and teeth of this species have been discovered so its existence is not in doubt. The species was assumed to have died out millions of years ago. But maybe it didn't? Perhaps the animals survived and spread out across the world before Asia became a separate continent.

It's hard to believe that such creatures are living beside us, undetected. However, as recently as 1938 a species of fish called the coelacanth was discovered swimming in the ocean, after being presumed extinct for millions of years! And the gorilla and giant panda were thought to be mythical creatures until they were discovered living deep in the forests. So maybe the suggestion isn't so crazy, after all.

If the animals really exist, it could explain why stories and beliefs about wild creatures which are half-ape, half-human, are so widespread in the folklore of many peoples. Native Americans see the giant creatures as caring 'brothers' who are aware that humans are hunting them and have worked out how to avoid capture. They only appear when they want to warn individuals, communities or humankind in general about some approaching danger.

But while stories of the Bigfoot are part of Native American folklore, there is, as yet, no definite physical evidence to prove their existence. There are no records of great apes or monkeys ever having inhabited America. No Bigfoot bones or bodies have ever been discovered there either. Unless such fossil remains are uncovered, the mystery will remain. The Bigfoot may be the product of wishful thinking, or exaggeration, or just a way to attract more tourists to a region. But life has a habit of surprising us ...

If these hairy giants are out there somewhere, we can be certain that they're shy and reclusive because they usually try to avoid all contact with humans. But from time to time people report that they have seen the 'monsters' in populated areas. If these giant cousins of ours really exist, it could be that they are just as curious about us as we are about them!

History

→ For exercises 1–4 see pages 120 and 124 in your Students' Book.

1 Complete the sentences with the correct form of the words in capitals.

1 Museum staff ......**threatened**...... to throw the children out of the museum if they didn't behave. THREAT
2 Archaeologists have discovered a large Viking .... site. BURY

3 Without a tomb to live in, the spirits of the pharaohs would be completely .... HOME
4 The teacher made us write an essay on Tutankhamen as a .... PUNISH
5 Last year I took part in a real-life .... EXCAVATE
6 We were so .... to find the Roman coins where we were digging! LUCK
7 On his ...., the king's body was carried to the cathedral. DIE
8 After invading London, the Romans slowly .... their hold on England. STRONG
9 The lecturer spoke on the subject at great .... LONG
10 There's a really interesting .... site near my town. ARCHAEOLOGY

2 Choose the correct noun to complete the sentences.

1 I've heard a *rumour/legend* that our history teacher is leaving soon.
2 The Romans rode in *thrones/chariots* pulled by horses.
3 Going on an archaeological dig can teach you a lot about the *history/story* of your country.
4 History is based on *statements/facts*, not fiction.
5 The place where the Archbishop died has become a *statue/shrine* which is often visited by pilgrims.

3 Choose the word that best completes the sentence.

1 Rabbits are small furry .**A**. .
   A animals   B beasts
2 My little brother wants me to tell him a bedtime ....
   A story   B account
3 Two men who made a ..... phone call to the police claiming they'd been chased by a 'yeti' ended up with a fine!
   A trick   B hoax
4 When I saw the elephant close up, I couldn't believe how ..... it was!
   A huge   B great
5 Scientists refuse to believe the creatures exist due to the complete ..... of evidence.
   A scarcity   B lack
6 John is really ..... and believes everything he's told.
   A credible   B gullible
7 People in many ancient civilisations invented ..... in order to explain natural or historical events.
   A fiction   B myths

4 Complete the sentences with the correct form of these verbs.

gaze   glare   peer   glimpse   ~~scan~~

1 I ....**scanned**......... the page for the date I was seeking.
2 Fred and his girlfriend sat in the café for hours .... dreamily into each other's eyes.
3 As the train raced along the track, we .... footprints in the snow.
4 Hearing a noise, the teacher .... angrily around the room.
5 The boy screwed up his eyes and .... through the keyhole, into the dark room.

More modal verbs

→ For exercise 1 see page 121 in your Students' Book.

1 Choose the correct form to complete the sentences.

A: Look! There's a huge bird on the roof of that building. It looks like a vulture!

B: Don't be daft! It 1) *can't be/mustn't be* a vulture. You 2) *must imagine/must be imagining* things!

A: No way! Come over here and look!

B: Wow, I see what you mean! What on earth is it doing here? 3) *Could it have escaped/Could it have been escaping* from a zoo, do you think?

A: No idea! I suppose it 4) *can be/may be* hungry. Shall we throw some food down for it?

B: Yeah, okay.

A: Well, someone, somewhere, 5) *must go/must be going* crazy looking for it. Should we phone the police or something?

B: Good thinking! I'll do that now, shall I?

Reporting verbs in the passive

→ For exercises 2–3 see page 125 in your Students' Book.

2 Complete the second sentences so it means the same as the first one.

1 They believe the Romans built this road.
The Romans ..... *are believed* ..... to
..... *have built* .... this road.

2 The first humans are said to have lived in trees.
It .... that the first humans
....

3 They claim that wolves are killing the sheep.
Wolves .... be
.... the sheep.

4 They think that a Viking burial ship is buried in this area.
A Viking burial ship .... buried in this area.

3 Rewrite the sentences using the words in capitals. Use between two and five words, including the word given.

1 It's not possible that they saw a wild ape in the USA.
HAVE
They *couldn't have seen* a wild ape in the USA.

2 People say humanoid creatures are living in the Himalayas.
TO
Humanoid creatures are .... in the Himalayas.

3 I suppose they were digging when they found the treasure.
MUST
They .... when they found the treasure.

4 They believe that the pharaoh died in winter.
IS
It .... the pharaoh died in winter.

5 It's possible that this pottery is Roman in origin.
BE
This pottery .... Roman in origin.

6 They think recent sightings of the yeti are false.
THOUGHT
Recent sightings of the yeti ....
false.

7 It's possible that his enemies murdered the king.
MAY
The king .... his enemies.

8 I don't believe you were listening just now.
CAN'T
You .... just now.

Use your English

1 **Complete the text with <u>one</u> word which best fits each gap.**

IS 'NESSIE' AN ELEPHANT?

1) ....A............ huge animal is rumoured to 2) .... living in Loch Ness, in Scotland. 'Loch' 3) .... a Scottish word meaning 'lake'. The water in Loch Ness is deep, cloudy, and extremely cold, 4) .... makes it hard to explore. The Loch's mystery inhabitant, 'Nessie', is said 5) .... have a huge body, a long neck and flippers. Some people think Nessie 6) .... be an ancient species of reptile, called a plesiosaur. But experts disagree, for two main reasons. First, plesiosaurs 7) .... believed to be extinct; they probably died out millions of years 8) .... Second, plesiosaurs were cold-blooded animals, so they could never 9) .... survived in the freezing waters of Loch Ness. Recently, it has been suggested that 'Nessie' could 10) .... an elephant! One expert pointed out that in the past, Nessie 11) .... often seen when a famous circus came to Scotland. The circus often stopped at the Loch 12) .... that the animals could cool down. The elephants often swam in the Loch. When an elephant is swimming, only 13) .... long trunk and two small humps (part of the head and back) can be seen. Might eyewitnesses have mistaken this for a monster?

2 **Choose the word or phrase that best completes the sentence.**

1 In class, we're studying ancient ..D.. .
  A stories   **B** facts
  C fiction   **D** history

2 The ground is very wet so it ..... during the night.
  A must be raining   **B** can rain
  C must have rained   **D** can have rained

3 The churchyard ..... to be haunted by ghosts but I don't believe it.
  A it is said   **B** is said
  C says   **D** said

4 The knife had made a large ..... in his chest.
  A injury   **B** damage
  C hurt   **D** wound

5 A crocodile is reported ..... people in a local swimming pool yesterday.
  A to have attacked   **B** to attack
  C it attacked   **D** having attacked

6 Many soldiers were killed in the battle but the king ..... .
  A outlived   **B** overcame
  C survived   **D** outlasted

7 You ..... for the history exam or you'd have got a better grade.
  A must have studied   **B** couldn't have studied
  C must study   **D** couldn't have been studying

8 The president is reported ..... in the Bahamas at the moment.
  A to holiday   **B** holidaying
  C he is holidaying   **D** to be holidaying

9 While they were ..... the ancient settlement, archaeologists found some priceless jewellery.
  A digging   **B** tunnelling
  C excavating   **D** burying

10 The Himalayas are supposed ..... home to the 'yeti' but scientists are not sure the creatures actually exist.
  A to be   **B** be
  C that they are   **D** being

11 The tomb was engraved with a curse, written in strange letters and ..... .
  A statues   **B** items
  C symbols   **D** charms

12 Some boys claimed there was a shark in the river but it turned out to be a ..... .
  A hoax   **B** play
  C laugh   **D** pretence

Writing *a story*

→ For exercises 1–7 see pages 126–127 in your Students' Book.

1 **Read the writing task and answer the questions to get ideas for your story.**

> You have been asked to write a story for a teen magazine. The story must end with the words: *'I know I didn't imagine it,'* Sarah told herself, *'but will anyone believe me?'*

1 Who was Sarah? How old was she? What kind of person was she?

2 Where was she when the event happened? (At home? On holiday? Somewhere else?) What was she doing?

3 What exactly happened? (Did she see something unusual or strange? Did she make a discovery?)

4 What happened next? What did she do? How did she feel?

5 How did the adventure end?

2 **Here is a possible paragraph plan for your story. Decide how you want to organise the ideas you had in Exercise 1, and complete the plan.**

> **Paragraph 1** (Introduction) ....
> **Paragraph 2** ....
> **Paragraph 3** ....
> **Paragraph 4** (Conclusion + prompt sentence from writing task) ....

3 **Use these notes to build up the first part of a story, using the correct past tenses.**

> Sarah/wake up/with a jump and/open/her eyes. Everyone in the tent/sleep. They/travel/all day. No wonder they were **tired**! Sarah/step/outside. She and her friends/chose/to camp near the forest because it/be/so **quiet**. But in the dark, it/look unwelcoming and **frightening**. She/get/back into the tent when she/suddenly hear/a **strange** noise. Something/move about/at the edge of the trees. The forest/say/be haunted. Feeling **scared**, Sarah peered into the darkness.

4 **Replace the adjectives in bold in Exercise 3 with these stronger adjectives.**

> bizarre   peaceful   terrified   exhausted   spooky

5 **Punctuate the next part of the story correctly.**

> At first she couldn't make out anything but as her eyes grew accustomed to the darkness she saw a huge shape is it animal or human she wondered she stood and watched as the thing came nearer it was huge and very hairy

6 **Choose the best ending for the story.**

1
> Sarah screamed and rushed to wake up her friends. But when they arrived, the 'thing' was gone.

2
> Then, just as she thought it would attack her, the creature turned and disappeared back into the forest. 'I know I didn't imagine it,' Sarah told herself, 'but will anyone believe me?'

3
> 'I can't believe what I'm seeing,' Sarah told herself.

7 **Now write your answer to the writing task in Exercise 1. Write about 120–180 words. Answer the following questions before you begin.**

1 Who is going to read your story?

2 Tick the things you should do when writing your story. Put a cross next to the things that you must <u>not</u> do.
   – use unusual and vivid adjectives
   – use the present perfect tense to relate finished events
   – forget who you are writing your story for
   – think of an interesting plot
   – make a plan before you start writing
   – divide your story into clear paragraphs, with an introduction, a middle and a conclusion
   – make the ending interesting/exciting
   – begin a new paragraph for each new sentence
   – use dialogue where appropriate, but not too much
   – check your spelling and punctuation when you've finished

3 How many paragraphs should you use for your story? Circle the correct answer.
   A one   **B** two   **C** three or more

Do you need more practice?
Go to: CD-ROM, Unit 11.

12 Get away!

Vocabulary

→ For exercises 1–3 see pages 128–129 in your Students' Book.

1 Complete the sentences with the correct words.

native   camping   coach   roller   ~~national~~
adventure   white-water   white-knuckle

1 The US government turned Yellowstone into a
......**national**........ park so it could preserve the
land and protect it from pollution.
2 We went to the fairground and went on some real
.... rides! I was petrified!
3 John loves doing .... sports like
rock-climbing and wind-surfing.
4 The most important .... equipment
you need is a tent!
5 The oak is a species of tree that is
.... to the UK.
6 If you're going .... rafting, don't
forget to wear a life jacket!
7 We took a .... drive round the city
centre so we could see all the sights.
8 Jenny had a ride on a .... coaster
and screamed all the way round!

**2 Complete the sentence with a suitable word. The
first letter has been given.**

1 You can't imagine how wonderful the
........**scenery**........ was – high mountains, green
valleys and amazing forests!
2 The young men dived off the top of the steep, rocky
c........................ that overhung the sea.
3 Our next d........................ is Paris, and we'll be
arriving there in 30 minutes.
4 Riding on a roller coaster is the most
e........................ feeling in the world!
5 Antarctica has never been developed – it's just one
great w........................!
6 Watching the volcano erupt was a really
a........................ experience!

**3 Complete the sentences with the correct form of
the words in brackets. Be careful! You may need to
use plural forms.**

1 You can take part in lots of ......**activities**......
(active) on the holiday, like surfing and hang-gliding.
2 It's the most .... (credible) place to
go rock-climbing!
3 We really liked our .... (instruct);
he was excellent.
4 Our hotel was really .... (luxury)
5 The forest is a .... (magic) place.
6 You'll see plenty of .... (wild) in
the forest, like bears and wolves.

Reading

**1 Read the text and choose the best answer, A, B, C
or D.**

1 Where can you take part in an activity that will benefit
the area you're visiting?
A Tortuguero Village   B Sarapiqui
C Arenal   D Danaus
2 What can you do in Arenal?
A jump off a volcano
B swim in warm water
C walk through the lava
D sleep under a starry sky
3 What does the brochure strongly recommend you do
in Tamarindo?
A stay in the hotel   B go shopping
C try surfing   D go horse-riding
4 Where can you find out about the efforts being made
to protect a species of reptile?
A Pirate's Beach   B Danaus
C Tortuguero Village   D Sarapiqui
5 Which of the following is not included in the price?
A riding gear   B camping costs
C museum fees   D pocket money
6 Where can you take part in some heart-stopping
activities before spending the night in a tent?
A Sarapiqui   B Tamarindo
C Pirate's Beach   D Tortuguero Village
7 How long is Costa Rica, according to the brochure?
A 762 miles   B 6%
C 845 km   D 200 km
8 In how many of the places do you stay in a hotel?
A 1   B 2   C 3   D 4

Home   Destinations   Plan your trip   Book   Gap year   Contact   Search   Watch

Costa Rica

Coasts, Canals and Canopies

Pulse rating: ♥ ♥ ♥ ♥

Come with us to explore stunning Costa Rica, a Central American paradise. It has 762 miles of coastline, 6% of the world's biodiversity, erupting volcanoes, thick rainforests, untouched sandy beaches and more than 845 species of birds. Not bad for a country barely 200 km long. On this holiday, you'll enjoy some of the best activities available in Central America!

Tortuguero

We drive through beautiful mountains and plantations to the Tortuguero Canals. Here, we take a two-hour boat trip to Mawamba Lodge, a country hotel where we will spend the night. On the way, we may see caimen (a small species of crocodile) basking or swimming in the clear water. The afternoon will be spent in Tortuguero Village, where we can explore the beach and learn about turtle conservation. An early morning boat trip the next day will give us the best chance of spotting monkeys, birds and iguanas in their natural habitat. Later we will hike into the rainforest to explore the flora and fauna. Those who are feeling energetic can take to the water again for a kayak trip.

Sarapiqui

Leaving the canals behind, we head inland to incredible Sarapiqui. On the way, we stop at the Museum of Indigenous Cultures to learn more about the local people. The following day is 'Adrenaline Day'! We set off early on a three-hour white-water rafting trip down the Sarapiqui River. Later we go horse-riding through the tropical rainforest, then fly on a zip wire through the forest canopy. That night we'll sleep under canvas in our forest camp so that you can hear the sounds of the rainforest at night.

Arenal

Arenal is awesome by day and jaw-dropping by night when the volcano spits out molten lava into the black Costa Rican sky! And you can see it all from the hottub in your luxury 5-star hotel room. Not a bad way to spend an evening! After eating, we trek towards the volcano, arriving at an awe-inspiring viewpoint in time to see the sun go down and the lava flow. We then head for a dip in the hot springs at the foot of the volcano.

Danaus

A visit to this Eco-Centre is optional. Costa Rica is at the forefront of responsible tourism and travel management. We're trying to play our part by encouraging our clients to get closely involved with local communities and conservation projects. If you volunteer for this activity, you'll be working with the local people and their children on a project to help the rainforest. We'll spend time planting trees and generally getting a bit dirty for a very worthwhile cause, as well as witnessing local lifestyles at close quarters.

Tamarindo

Today we head to the Pacific Coast. Our luxury hotel is just a two-minute woodland stroll from the secluded beach. In this surfer's paradise it is almost compulsory to have a go at riding the Pacific waves. The hotel can arrange lessons or you can try one of the many surf schools. Alternatively, you can shop to your heart's content, kayak, or simply relax by the pool.

Pirate's Beach

We drive in convoy along off-road trails, crossing rivers, visiting small Costa Rican villages and stopping to admire the wildlife before reaching the stunning white sands and palm trees of Pirate's Beach. Here you can kayak, snorkel and swim in the turquoise waters of the Pacific Ocean while our guides prepare lunch.

Accommodation:
We use a variety of accommodation from luxury 5-star hotels to tented rainforest camps.

What's included in the price?
– *Return flights*
– *Accommodation*
– *Rainforest Boat Trip. Tortuguero Village Tour. Turtle Conservation Centre Visit. Tortuguero Exploration (boat trip, hike). Museum of Indigenous Cultures. Rainforest Project.*
– *All equipment, instruction and supervision from guides and activity providers*
– *All transport between locations and activities*

Holidays

→ For exercises 1–5 see pages 130 and 134 in your Students' Book.

1 Match the words (1–10) with the words (a–j) to make compound words. Be careful! Some are written as two words, some as one word and some are hyphenated.

1	sun	a	climbing
2	life	b	set
3	rock	c	gliding
4	scuba	d	jacket
5	shopping	e	mall
6	sight	f	park
7	hang	g	seeing
8	theme	h	seeker
9	thrill	i	diving
10	wet	j	suit

2 Complete the sentences with compound words.

1 Sorry I'm late but I got caught in a terrible traffic .... jam ....
2 Before you get on the plane, you have to show your boarding ....
3 You can buy a travel ticket from the booking ....
4 Air passengers have to wait in the departure .... for their flight to be called.
5 Shall I put your suitcase up on the luggage .... for you?
6 If you're going on a walking holiday, you'll need to carry your things in a back ....

3 Choose the correct preposition to complete the sentences.

1 The staff in our hotel worked all night so they could provide service .B. the clock.
   A over   **B** around
2 I wouldn't dare go on holiday ..... my own!
   A on   **B** by
3 Hollywood is famous ..... movie-making.
   A for   **B** at
4 Tomorrow, we're ..... on holiday.
   A off   **B** out
5 Our hotel is situated ..... the outskirts of the city.
   A in   **B** on
6 We can get to the city centre ..... foot.
   A on   **B** by

4 Complete each set of sentences with the correct words.

1 **tour/travel/journey**
   a To reach our campsite, we had to make a long train .... journey ....
   b As part of our holiday, we went on a .... of a safari park.
   c If you're planning to .... on the roads tonight, watch out for the fog.

2 **road/path/way**
   a Do you know the best .... to get to the theme park?
   b You should never cross the .... without looking, especially in the city centre.
   c We discovered a grassy .... through the woods.

3 **scene/scenery/view**
   a From our window, we got a marvellous .... of the cathedral.
   b As our train crossed the mountains, we saw plenty of amazing ....
   c Police have cordoned off the .... of the accident.

5 Complete the sentences with a suitable preposition. You can use the same preposition more than once.

1 He blamed me .... for .... losing the tickets.
2 Did you succeed .... getting a refund?
3 Maria insisted .... going to the beach.
4 We can't rely .... the buses to be on time.
5 I'm ashamed .... letting you down so badly.
6 I've applied .... a visa to visit the USA.
7 Simon got involved .... an argument on the beach yesterday.
8 My little sister is afraid .... the dark.
9 Guests are complaining .... the noise in the hotel.
10 I know I can depend .... you.

Relative clauses

➜ For exercise 1–2 see page 131 in your Students' Book.

1 Choose the word or phrase that best completes the sentence.

1 I've just met a boy .B. father owns a big hotel in town.
  A whom
  B whose
  C that
  D who

2 The photo ..... was taken in Mexico.
  A at which you're looking
  B who you're looking at
  C that you're looking
  D you're looking at

3 Tents are canvas sheets ..... to sleep in.
  A they are used
  B of use
  C used
  D who are used

4 We're looking for a resort ..... we can do lots of activities.
  A where
  B which
  C how
  D why

5 We saw a live volcano, ... was awesome!
  A that
  B it
  C which
  D who

6 The stores ..... were quite expensive!
  A we shopped
  B which we shopped
  C who we shopped
  D we shopped at

2 Join each pair of sentences using a relative clause. Use a relative pronoun where necessary.

1 The castle was destroyed in the 15th century. We visited it on day two of our holiday.
2 They've managed to book the holiday. They wanted to go on it.
3 Can you see the bird? I'm looking at it.
4 They camped out in the rainforest. That was the best part of their holiday.
5 Have you seen the guide? He's supposed to take us round.
6 I'm staying with a friend. Her relatives own a yacht.
7 We went to a theme park. It was a brilliant experience.
8 Yellowstone is home to a great number of bears. It's a national park.

Present participles verb-*ing*

➜ For exercise 3 see page 135 in your Students' Book.

3 Complete the second sentence so it means the same as the first one.

1 First we ate lunch and then we went to the beach.
   After eating lunch, we went to the beach .
2 We realised we'd missed our flight so we went home.
   Realising ....
3 She had never been on a roller coaster before so she was a bit nervous.
   Having ....
4 We saw a wild bear near our tents so we ran away.
   Seeing ....
5 Because we were first in the queue, we got a good seat on the coach.
   Being ....
6 First he won the competition, then he bought himself a surfboard.
   After ....

Use your English

1 Complete the text with <u>one</u> word that best fits each gap.

NEW YORK

THE BIG APPLE

New York, the city 1) ....in............ which I live, has 2) .... inhabitants than any other US city. 3) .... was originally called 'New Amsterdam' but was renamed by the British 4) .... they conquered the city in 1664. Our city has many landmarks which are 5) .... to people all over the world. The Statue of Liberty greeted people 6) .... came to the USA a century ago. Wall Street is 7) .... bankers and financiers do business. Central Park is a peaceful area that's great 8) .... relax in. The headquarters of the United Nations is here, too, 9) .... is why there are so many international diplomats in the city. New York has great theatres, many 10) .... which are on Broadway. And when it comes to sport, there are 11) .... of great facilities. Baseball is the 12) .... closely followed sport in the city and we have two big teams. Finally, people 13) .... money to spend can go to Fifth Avenue, which is where the top department stores are to be found.

2 Read the text and choose the best answer, A, B, C or D.

Over recent decades, it 1) ..D.. become trendy for teenagers 2) ..... are between school and university to take 3) ..... year out from studying. Some go on long train 4) ..... round Europe. Others go further, backpacking or hitchhiking to countries 5) ..... Thailand or India. Cheap travel isn't always comfortable or convenient. The kind of hostels backpackers have to stay 6) ..... aren't always ideal and it may be necessary to check for spiders and scorpions before 7) ..... the bathroom! But the travellers get to visit fantastic places, meet interesting people and 8) ..... enormous fun. Of course, school-leavers who have a conscience want to give back to the countries they visit, 9) ..... is why today's backpackers often take part in a volunteer project along the way. For a fee, travel companies will arrange 10) ..... students to work on a turtle conservation project, for example, or to teach English in poor villages. However, some experts see all this as a 11) ..... of time. They say the only people who really benefit are the travel companies. Clearly anyone 12) ..... a gap year needs to think about these matters very carefully before they 13) ..... off.

1	**A** was	**B** had	**C** is	**D** has
2	**A** who	**B** whose	**C** whom	**D** when
3	**A** the	**B** a	**C** an	**D** some
4	**A** travels	**B** excursions	**C** journeys	**D** tours
5	**A** so	**B** like	**C** such	**D** as
6	**A** at	**B** on	**C** by	**D** for
7	**A** used	**B** to use	**C** use	**D** using
8	**A** have	**B** do	**C** find	**D** make
9	**A** which	**B** it	**C** this	**D** that
10	**A** that	**B** how	**C** for	**D** if
11	**A** waste	**B** loss	**C** ruin	**D** misuse
12	**A** takes	**B** taking	**C** took	**D** taken
13	**A** put	**B** go	**C** set	**D** leave

Writing *an article*

➜ For exercises 1–8 see pages 136–137 in your Students' Book.

1 **Read the writing task below. Then answer the questions.**

You read this announcement in a teen magazine:

> **DREAM HOLIDAYS FOR TEENAGERS**
> Can you recommend a holiday that's great for teenagers? We'd like to hear from you.
> Write us an article
> – describing the holiday.
> – saying why it would appeal especially to teenagers.

Write your article in 120–180 words.

1 Who is going to read your article?
2 Should your style be very formal or lively and chatty?
3 What two things must your article include?

2 **Make a list of notes about a holiday that's good for teenagers. Include:**

– where the holiday place is and how to get there.
– two or three things you can do or see there.
– reasons why it's so good for teenagers.

3 **Choose the best introduction for the article.**

1
> Last year I went to ... . It was very enjoyable.

2
> If you want a great holiday, I recommend spending a week in ... . If you're a teenager, you'll find it's the best holiday ever!

4 **Read this part of an article about a dream holiday and divide it into two paragraphs. Then underline the topic sentence in each paragraph.**

> ... Kruger Park is in the north-east of South Africa. To get there, you have to fly to Johannesburg, then change flights. It's a long journey but very worthwhile! The Park is awesome. It covers a huge area, and a lot of it is parched dry in summer. It's home to lions, elephants, rhinos and lots more wildlife, which you can see when you go on safari. The best way to get about is on the back of an elephant! You feel really safe up there, and none of the animals you want to see are scared of you. You can feed your elephant too, and swim with it – it's really good fun!

5 **Read these two possible conclusions for the article in Exercise 4. Tick the best one.**

1
> There are plenty of other things to do as well, like learning to abseil in the mountains or canoeing down the river. Everywhere you go, you see spectacular scenery and incredible wildlife. It's a dream holiday no teenager should miss!

2
> I recommend this holiday to all teenagers.

6 **Choose the best title for the article in Exercise 4.**
1 My dream holiday
2 Safari adventure

7 **Make a paragraph plan for your article in Exercise 1. You will need three paragraphs at least.**

Paragraph 1 ....
Paragraph 2 ....
Paragraph 3 ....
Paragraph 4 ....

8 **Now write your answer to the writing task in Exercise 1. Remember to include a title!**

Grammar

1 Choose the correct word or words to complete the sentences.

1 Someone *can/must* have taken your phone. It's not in your bag!
2 Having *lost/losing* his passport, he was unable to board the plane.
3 I saw Tony this morning so he can't *go/have gone* on holiday!
4 Mexico is supposed *being/to be* an exciting country to visit.
5 We went to see the Acropolis, *which/that* was really amazing.
6 Do you know *who's/whose* bag this is?
7 The holiday, *which/that* we booked last week, has been cancelled.
8 Despite *getting/to get* homesick, I enjoyed my holiday very much.

2 Complete the text with <u>one</u> word which best fits each gap.

Tourist companies in Egypt must 1) ....have.......... been delighted when the results of a new survey were published yesterday. According to the survey, which set out to discover the 'new seven wonders of the world', visiting 2) ....Pyramids is most people's number one dream travel experience. The Australian tourist industry can't 3) ....too disappointed either, as the second dream destination was the Great Barrier Reef. The Reef, 4) .... divers can swim through coral and enjoy stunning underwater views, was a hit with 5) .... than 40% of the parents and kids who took part 6) ....the survey.
Going on safari in Kenya was a hit with those people 7) ....want to get up close and personal with wild animals. It came third in the survey. Sledging in Greenland, 8) ....was chosen by 28% of families, was the fourth most popular kind of holiday. Cowboy ranching holidays 9) ....the USA came fifth. The final choices were a visit to the Great Wall of China, and visiting the legendary Aztec temples in Mexico. And who was everybody's dream guide? TV chef Jamie Oliver, 10) ....face is familiar to television audiences around the country, was 11) ....of the most wanted tour guides on everybody's dream holiday. Unfortunately for some, Jamie is not thought 12) ....be in favour of a career move just yet!

3 Rewrite the sentences using the words in capitals. Use between two and five words, including the word given.

1 I don't believe it's possible that a spaceship has landed in the USA.
HAVE
A spaceship ..*can't have landed*.. in the USA.

2 People believe that the Romans built this settlement.
THAT
It .... the Romans built this settlement.

3 I've never eaten in a better restaurant than Georgio's.
EVER
Georgio's is the best restaurant ....

4 It's pretty clear that they were flying over the Atlantic when the storm broke.
MUST
They .... over the Atlantic when the storm broke.

5 She went on holiday even though she had just failed her exams.
FAILED
Despite ...., she still went on holiday.

6 Experts say that tourists are growing tired of beach holidays.
TO
Tourists are .... tired of beach holidays.

7 Can you identify the owner of this jacket?
WHOSE
Do you know ....?

8 I spoke to a very helpful courier.
WAS
The courier .... very helpful.

Vocabulary

4 **Write a compound word for each definition below.**

1 area where people can stay in tents or caravans
.... campsite ....
2 thing you get into and zip up when you're camping in a tent ....
3 place where you report your arrival and hand over your luggage at an airport ....
4 long line of vehicles on a road that cannot move
....
5 bag used to carry things on your back, especially when you go walking ....
6 street on which cars can only go in one direction
....
7 the sport of jumping from a plane with a parachute
....
8 card or pass you must show in order to get on a plane
....

5 **Complete the sentences with the correct form of the words in capitals.**

1 Their ...... behaviour .... was so bad they were thrown off the coach.   BEHAVE
2 That historian has an amazing .... of knowledge of ancient history.   BROAD
3 Experts discouraged onlookers from entering the .... chamber.   BURY
4 The idea that there are alligators living under our city is beyond ....   BELIEVE
5 The ancient .... was home to about a thousand people.   SETTLE
6 I didn't have enough .... to lift the fossil off the beach.   STRONG
7 After the .... of the king, his son took his place on the throne.   DIE
8 The mummy lay .... in the tomb for thousands of years until the archaeologists discovered it.   DISTURB

6 **Choose the correct word to complete the sentences.**

1 My brother likes factual books but I prefer *myth/fiction*.
2 The soldier was buried in a simple, unmarked *tomb/ shrine*.
3 The ancient Romans drove *thrones/chariots* pulled by horses.
4 Someone told me Jane had won the lottery but it was just a *legend/rumour*.
5 A man claimed to have found a dinosaur living in the mountains but it was a *hoax/trick*, of course.
6 Tomorrow, we're setting out on a long *travel/journey*.
7 Buckingham Palace is *placed/situated* in the middle of London.
8 We're planning to *do/go* sightseeing tomorrow.

7 **Complete the sentences with a suitable preposition.**

1 I wasn't involved .... in .... planning the holiday.
2 He blamed his friend .... missing the plane.
3 My brother is scared .... flying.
4 On the cruise ship, you could see live entertainment .... the clock.
5 Our hotel was .... the outskirts of the city.
6 Our courier advised us .... the best places to visit.
7 At our campsite, there were people from all .... the world.
8 We found we couldn't rely .... the train service to get around the country.

Words that go together

Adjective + preposition

about
angry about
annoyed about
anxious about
careful about
certain about
concerned about
confident about
confused about
crazy about
delighted about
disappointed about
enthusiastic about
excited about
furious about
happy about
nervous about
pleased about
right about
serious about
sorry about
sure about
upset about
worried about
wrong about

at
amazed at
amused at
arrive at
bad at
brilliant at
excellent at
good at
hopeless at
shocked at
skilled at
surprised at
terrible at
upset at
useless at

by
amazed by
amused by
impressed by
shocked by
surprised by
upset by

for
bad for
famous for

late for
lucky for
necessary for
ready for
responsible for
sorry for

of
afraid of
ashamed of
aware of
capable of
certain of
critical of
envious of
fond of
frightened of
full of
guilty of
independent of
jealous of
scared of
short of
suspicious of
tired of
typical of

on
dependent on
keen on
reliant on

to
accustomed to
addicted to
engaged to
generous to
inferior to
kind to
married to
nice to
polite to
related to
responsible to
rude to
sensitive to
similar to

with
angry with
annoyed with
bored with
busy with
careful with
content with
crowded with

delighted with
disappointed with
familiar with
friendly with
furious with
happy with
impressed with
involved with
occupied with
pleased with
satisfied with
upset with

Verb + preposition

about
advise sb about sth
agree (with sb) about sth
argue (with sb) about sth
ask sb about sb/sth
care about
complain about
disagree (with sb) about sth
dream about
forget about
joke about sth (with sb)
learn about
protest about
quarrel (with sb) about sth
remind sb about sth
sympathise (with sb) about sth
talk about sth (with sb)
tell sb about sth
think about
warn sb about sth
write about

against
compete against
protest against
warn sb against sth

for
apologise for
apply for
arrest sb for sth
ask sb for sth
blame sb for sth
criticise sb for sth
forgive sb for sth
hope for
look for
prepare for
provide for
search for
thank sb for sth

from
benefit from
borrow sth from sb
come from
differ from
disappear from
escape from
hear from sb
prevent sb from doing sth
protect sb from sb/sth
recover from
resign from
save sb from sth
steal sth from sb

in
arrive in
believe in
end in
persist in
result in
succeed in (doing sth)

into
break into
change sth into sth
crash into
divide sth into sth

of
accuse sb of sth
approve of
consist of
die of
dream of
hear of
think of
warn sb of sth

on
advise sb on sth
agree on sth
bet on
blame sth on sb
concentrate on
congratulate sb on sth
count on
decide on
depend on
improve on
insist on
rely on
spend (time/money) on sth
waste (time/money) on sth

to

apologise to sb (for/about sth)
belong to
compare sb/sth to sb/sth
connect sth to sth
explain sth to sb
happen to
introduce sb to sb
lead sb to
listen to
object to
prefer sth/sb to sth/sb
react to
reply to
see to
speak to
talk to
write to

with

agree with sb (about sth)
argue with sb (on/about sth)
collide with
communicate with
compare sb/sth with sb/sth
compete with
connect with
cope with
deal with
disagree with sb (about sth)
discuss sth with sb
fight with
fill sth with sth
joke with sb (about sth)
live with
provide sb with sth
quarrel with sb (about sth)
share sth with sb
sympathise with

Verbs + verb -ing

admit
adore
avoid
can't face
can't help
can't stand
carry on
consider
delay
deny
detest
dislike
dread
enjoy
fancy

feel like
finish
give up
go on
hate
imagine
keep
mention
mind
miss
postpone
practise
put off
recall
recommend
resent
risk
suggest

Verbs + object + to + infinitive

advise
allow
cause
encourage
force
get
invite
order
persuade
remind
teach
tell
warn

Verbs + to + infinitive

agree
arrange
ask
can't afford
can't wait
choose
decide
expect
fail
forget
help
hope
intend
learn
manage
mean
need

offer
plan
prepare
pretend
promise
refuse
tend
try
want
would hate
would like
would love
would prefer

Verbs + -ing or to + infinitive (change in meaning)

forget
go on
like
mean
regret
remember
stop
try

Forming nouns

Verbs + suffixes:

-al
survive – survival
bury – burial
-ance
perform – performance
-ence
obey – obedience
-ion/-sion
decide – decision
destroy – destruction
discuss – discussion
-ment
entertain – entertainment
improve – improvement
-ness
forgive – forgiveness
-nt
participate – participant
-ty/-iety
save – safety
vary – variety
-ure
please – pleasure
-y
discover – discovery

-er/-or
employ – employer
sail – sailor
-ee
employ – employee
-f
believe – belief
live – life
prove – proof

Other ways to form nouns from verbs:
behave – behaviour
choose – choice
die – death
fly – flight
laugh – laughter
marry – marriage
succeed – success

Adjectives + suffixes:
-ance/-ence
important – importance
obedient – obedience
intelligent – intelligence
-cy
accurate – accuracy
fluent – fluency
-ion/-ation
aggressive – aggression
determined – determination
-ness
bright – brightness
happy – happiness
-th
warm – warmth
long – length
broad – breadth
strong – strength
true – truth
-ty/-ity/-iety
loyal – loyalty
able – ability
various – variety
-y
difficult – difficulty
brave – bravery

Forming adjectives

Verbs/nouns + suffixes:
-able/-ible
enjoy – enjoyable
horror – horrible
-al
survive – survival
environment – environmental
-ed
tire – tired
-ent/-ant
efficiency – efficient
please – pleasant
-ful
care – careful
-ic/-ical
sympathy – sympathetic
critic – critical
-ing
amuse – amusing
-ish
style – stylish
-ive
expense – expensive
-less
hope – hopeless
-ous
danger – dangerous
glamour – glamorous
-y
guilt – guilty
fun – funny

Forming verbs

Adjectives/nouns + '-en':
broad – broaden
strong/strength – strengthen
long/length – lengthen

Prefix 'en-':
en-
danger – endanger
able – enable

Opposites

Prefixes to make words negative:
un- + *adjective/verb/noun*
    unhappy
    undo
    unemployment
dis- + *adjective/verb/noun*
    disobedient
    dislike
    disorganisation

il- (+-l) + *adjective/noun*
    illegal
    illiterate
im- (+-m/-p) + *adjective/noun*
    immoral
    impossible
    imperfection
in + *adjective/noun*
    incomplete
    inattention
ir- (+-r) + *adjective/noun*
    irrational
    irregularity

Compound words

Compound adjectives:

adjective + noun
a fast-food restaurant
noun + adjective
duty-free goods
adjective/adverb + *-ing*
good-looking
easy-going
adjective/adverb + past participle
old-fashioned
bad-tempered
grey-haired

Compound nouns:

noun + noun
website
roller coaster
pop singer
mobile phone
noun + *-ing*
skate-boarding
rock-climbing
***-ing* + noun**
booking office
swimming costume

Other combinations:
make-up
father-in-law
sunshine
a passer-by
white-water rafting
a windbreak

Answer key

Unit 1

Vocabulary 1

1
1	on	**2**	about
3	from	**4**	in
5	on	**6**	of
7	of	**8**	in
9	to	**10**	to
11	for	**12**	for

2
1	dull	**2**	sincere
3	severe	**4**	natural
5	cynical	**6**	brilliant
7	unaffected		

Reading

1   **1** B   **2** C   **3** A   **4** A   **5** D   **6** C   **7** B   **8** B

Vocabulary 2

1
1	audience	**2**	contestant
3	gig	**4**	stardom
5	stadium	**6**	performance
7	album	**8**	audition
9	tour	**10**	talent

2
1	A	**2**	B
3	A	**4**	B
5	A	**6**	B
7	B	**8**	A
9	B		

3
1	for	**2**	out
3	up	**4**	along
5	through	**6**	back

4
1	broaden	**2**	entertainment
3	sensational	**4**	youth
5	arrival	**6**	popularity
7	strengthen	**8**	enable
9	careful	**10**	happiness

Grammar

1
1	C	**2**	A
3	C	**4**	B
5	B	**6**	A
7	C	**8**	A

2
1	have spent	**2**	Have you been crying?
3	do you think	**4**	have been practising
5	Have you listened	**6**	are always complaining
7	have just finished	**8**	look

3
1	has been singing	**2**	has performed
3	has been	**4**	has never played
5	has managed	**6**	follows
7	perform	**8**	vote
9	is fighting	**10**	wants
11	is working	**12**	goes
13	gets	**14**	has worked
15	believes	**16**	hopes

4   **1** A   **2** B   **3** B   **4** B   **5** B   **6** A

Use your English

1
1	wonderful	**2**	dancers
3	sensational	**4**	well
5	live	**6**	famous
7	singers	**8**	really
9	interesting	**10**	popularity
11	successful		

2
1	has been singing for	**2**	seldom takes part in
3	has not phoned me for	**4**	have been (dancing)
5	doesn't like	**6**	have never been to/visited
7	since he sang	**8**	are always criticising

Writing *a letter of application*

1   **1** b)   **2** b)   **3** a)   **4** b)

2   b, d, f, h, i

3   (*Students' own answers*)

4
1 I'm writing to you about the TV talent show you are organising.
2 I can sing and dance and I play lead guitar as well.
3 I have been studying music and dance for three years now.
4 This year, I have performed in public a number of times.
5 I belong to a dance club and we give shows very often.

5   1, 3, 5, 7

6   (*Students' own answers*)

Unit 2

Vocabulary 1

1
1	struggled	**2**	survive
3	rush	**4**	lifted
5	dig	**6**	grabbed
7	resemble	**8**	grip
9	disturb	**10**	strike

Answer key

2
1 thrilling   2 terrified
3 dirty   4 natural
5 bleed   6 decision
7 appearance   8 impossible

3
1 with   2 of
3 up   4 from
5 of   6 in
7 of   8 to
9 of   10 from
11 for   12 in

4
1 find out   2 turn into
3 go for   4 calm down
5 go back

Reading

1
1 H   2 E   3 B   4 G   5 C   6 F   7 D
Sentence A is not needed.

Vocabulary 2

1
Mammal = leopard, gorilla
Reptile/Amphibian = frog, turtle
Arachnid = scorpion, spider
Bird = parrot, eagle
Fish/Shellfish = shark, crab, turtle, salmon

2
1 lightning   2 drought
3 heat wave   4 gale
5 earthquake   6 flood
7 breeze   8 environment

3
1 come off   2 come from
3 come back   4 come about
5 come up   6 come across

4
1 change   2 reefs
3 animals   4 gases
5 industry   6 layer
7 wave   8 warming

5
1 d   2 f   3 g   4 e   5 a   6 b   7 h   8 c

6
1 at   2 to
3 under   4 by
5 about   6 in

Grammar

1
1 became   2 thought
3 was driving   4 was waiting
5 saw   6 hadn't noticed
7 was following   8 spotted
9 was sitting   10 ran
11 jumped   12 hid
13 arrived   14 got off
15 had been travelling   16 had discovered

2
1 while we were visiting
2 had not been/flown in
3 used to ride
4 It had been snowing/It had snowed during
5 had already finished

3
1 the   2 -
3 a   4 the
5 a   6 the
7 the   8 a
9 -   10 a
11 -   12 the

Use your English

1
1 C   2 D   3 B   4 C   5 D   6 D   7 B   8 A
9 C   10 D   11 A

2
1 for   2 used
3 but/until   4 was
5 when   6 been
7 the   8 were
9 had   10 a
11 While/As   12 into/across
13 them

Writing *a story*

1 (*Students' own answers*)

2
Paragraph 1 give your story a dramatic opening …
Paragraph 2 paint the background …
Paragraph 3 describe the main events …
Paragraph 4 round off …

3
1 Suddenly   2 loudly
3 anxiously   4 extremely
5 quietly   6 confidently
7 Unfortunately

4 The next morning, we got up very early.
None of us had been sailing before so we did not know what to pack.
While we were putting our things into the car, Mum hurried to the local shops.
She came back with a large packet of sea-sickness pills, a torch and a new mobile phone.
We all giggled when we saw her – but we did not laugh for long!

5 (*Students' own answers*)

Time to revise 1

Grammar

1
1 am standing
2 have just arrived
3 normally work
4 made
5 chose
6 goes out
7 have been practising
8 have to
9 have never been
10 have clearly been dancing
11 have already learned
12 looks like

2 1 B 2 D 3 A 4 C 5 A 6 D 7 D 8 D
9 A 10 C

3
1 was   2 in
3 been   4 of
5 he   6 a
7 the   8 Since
9 won/obtained/got 10 as
11 not   12 enjoys/loves/likes

Vocabulary

4
1 An eagle is a species of bird and has feathers and claws.
2 A shark is a species of fish and has fins.
3 A butterfly is a species of insect and has wings and six legs.
4 A turtle is a species of reptile and has a shell.
5 A tiger is a species of mammal and has thick fur.

5

	noun	adjective	verb
1	care	*careful/careless*	*care*
2	*terror*	*terrified/terrifying*	terrify
3	*life*	living	*live*
4	*competition*	*competitive*	compete
5	strength	*strong*	*strengthen*
6	*success*	successful	*succeed*
7	*safety*	*safe*	save
8	*entertainment*	entertaining	*entertain*
9	ability	*able/capable*	*enable*
10	*popularity*	*popular*	popularise

6
1 entertainment   2 strengthen
3 succeed   4 safety
5 enabled   6 live
7 competitive   8 popularity
9 terrified   10 careless

7
1 of   2 about
3 of   4 at
5 in   6 of
7 in   8 at
9 of/about   10 to

8 1 D 2 C 3 B 4 A 5 D 6 C 7 D 8 A
9 B 10 C

Unit 3

Vocabulary 1

1
1 variety   2 exciting
3 personality   4 director
5 decisions   6 comfortable
7 competition   8 practical

2
1 useful   2 trying
3 cool   4 stiff
5 varied   6 sociable
7 nerve-wracking

3
1 in   2 on
3 on   4 in
5 about   6 to
7 into   8 out
9 in   10 out

Reading

1 1 A 2 C 3 B 4 B 5 A 6 D 7 B

Vocabulary 2

1
1 employer   2 retire
3 promote   4 work
5 earn   6 contract

2
1 presenter   2 applicants
3 qualifications 4 application
5 promotion   6 employees
7 unemployed   8 training
9 specialise   10 varied

3
1 on   2 at
3 behind   4 under
5 on   6 out of

4 1 B 2 B 3 A 4 A 5 B 6 A

5
1 over   2 on
3 in   4 up
5 off   6 out

6
1 risk   2 prospects
3 grips   4 graduation
5 security

Answer key

Grammar

1 1 B 2 A 3 A 4 B 5 B 6 B 7 A 8 A
9 A 10 B 11 A 12 B

2 1 leave 2 am doing
3 have had 4 arrives
5 get

3 1 are you going to do 2 'll look for
3 'm going to do 4 'm going to take
5 'll go/'m going 6 'll travel
7 will be living 8 will have done
9 will be 10 Shall I ask

4 1 by the time 2 while
3 until 4 as soon as

Use your English

1 1 active 2 completely
3 fitness 4 ability
5 entertainer 6 extremely
7 unlimited 8 retirement
9 trainer 10 encouragement
11 instructions

2 1 we will have set up
2 until I send in
3 am going to (attend/start/apply to)
4 will be fifteen on
5 are you doing anything/what are you doing
6 will be travelling
7 after I've discussed it
8 while you're having

3 1 time 2 have
3 be 4 are
5 will 6 to
7 soon/long 8 When/After/Once
9 until 10 going
11 done/completed

Writing *an informal letter*

1 1 Your friend/Steve
2 friendly
3 (Open answer)
4 (Suggested answer) It helps you communicate.
5 (Open answer)
6 (Open answer)

2 1 Say which type of job Steve should choose (fruit-picking or hospital cleaner) and give reasons why.
2 Say Steve should stay with a family and give reasons why.
3 Say what the weather's like in the summer.
4 Say I can't spend a weekend with Steve in August and apologise and explain why.

3 Great to hear from you!
If I were you, I'd get a job in a hospital. You'll get lots more chance to practise the language that way.
The weather's usually great in summer so no worries there!
I'm really sorry but I won't be able to see you in August because I'll be abroad.

4 Personal plans = future with *going to*
Fixed or scheduled events in the future = present continuous
Ideas about the future that you're not sure about= future with *will*

5 (*Suggested answer*)
Paragraph 1 Thanks for letter. Glad you're coming …
Paragraph 2 which type of job you should choose (fruit-picking or hospital cleaner) and why
Paragraph 3 why you should stay with a family
Paragraph 4 what the weather's like in the summer …
Paragraph 5 sorry I can't spend a weekend with you because …
Closing (Write back soon!)

6 (*Students' own answers*)

Unit 4

Vocabulary 1

1 1 d 2 g 3 e 4 i 5 j 6 f 7 h 8 c
9 a 10 b

2 1 strict 2 disrespectful
3 nasty 4 homesick
5 rebellious 6 isolated
7 confused 8 badly behaved

3 1 in 2 into
3 out of 4 in
5 around 6 in
7 in 8 in

Reading

1 1 F: Mark's been at Red Forest for eighteen months now and will reach the end of his course soon.
2 C: Luckily for Mark, his parents decided against boot camp when they read a report on the subject. This made it clear that boot camps just don't work.
3 E: While students are expected to work hard at their academic studies during the week, weekends are much more relaxed. It's the time for hobbies and special interests! Off-campus activities include rafting and mountain-biking.
4 B: Anyone caught breaking a rule, however small, has to do hard physical work as punishment.

92

5 D: The teenagers also have counselling sessions several times a week, as individuals and in groups, where they get help with any emotional issues that are troubling them.

6 F: Before he finishes, he'll be taking part in three weeks of voluntary activities – maybe working with homeless people or at an animal shelter.

7 A: Mark has a lot in common with the teenagers at Red Forest school in Colorado.

8 D: The staff are caring and supportive and give students lots of positive encouragement to achieve their dreams.

9 B: It's a bit like being in the army. You start the day with an early morning wake-up call and are then made to run several kilometres before breakfast! There is military-style discipline.

10 E: Climbing with his peers has taught him the importance of cooperation and teamwork, as well.

11 A: They had no direction in life and didn't understand the bad effect they were having on themselves, their family or friends.

12 C: Teenagers, it seems, refuse to listen to authority figures they don't respect. It's the same with rules – if teenagers think they're unfair, they won't obey them.

13 D: It's a boarding school, so students eat and sleep there and only go home for the holidays.

14 F: I didn't believe I could achieve anything much. This school has shown me I really can achieve my dreams if I want to. It's up to me to make something of my life. I know that now.

15 A: They'd made a habit of bullying their schoolmates and disobeying their teachers, and had driven their parents crazy with their bad behaviour.

16 E: Learning to rock climb has given him a great sense of accomplishment and helped his self-confidence.

Vocabulary 2

1 **1** moody **2** generous
3 arrogant **4** spoiled
5 rude **6** stubborn

2 **1** girlfriend **2** niece
3 cousins **4** guardian
5 step- **6** widow
7 great- **8** nephew

3 **1** B **2** A **3** B **4** A **5** A **6** A

4 **1** nagging **2** respect
3 lose **4** bullied
5 arguing

5 **1** off **2** out
3 down **4** on
5 out **6** in
7 up **8** up

6 **1** doing **2** make
3 doing **4** do
5 make **6** made
7 do **8** make

Grammar

1 **1** must **2** should have been cutting
3 don't have to **4** didn't have to repeat
5 should **6** needn't
7 ought to **8** have to

2 **1** can't, have **2** Can, can't
3 had to, could **4** should
5 didn't need/have to **6** mustn't
7 couldn't **8** needn't have

3 **1** needn't have apologised
2 you need to get
3 have/'ve got to keep
4 didn't have to pay
5 need not/n't have worried
6 must not/had better not break
7 shouldn't have done
8 might have had

Use your English

1 **1** can **2** have/need
3 must **4** told
5 could **6** to
7 not **8** ought
9 had **10** did
11 able

2 **1** C **2** D **3** A **4** C **5** D **6** D **7** B **8** A
9 B **10** B **11** C

Writing *an informal letter*

1 **1** A girl from his street.
2 No, because he's scared what will happen.
3 *(Open answer)*
4 *(Open answer)*

2 *(Open answer)*

3 **1** First, you could decide to say nothing./ Second, you could tell the girl how you feel.
2 That's probably not a good idea because you'll never get to date the girl./ I think this is a much better solution as at least you'll know the truth.
3 I'm sorry to hear you're going through such a tough time. /But don't worry – things are never as bad as they seem.

4 You must …

5 **1** The letter of reply contains four paragraphs.
Paragraph 1 = Introduction – reassurance
Paragraph 2 = suggestion 1 – say nothing, what might happen
Paragraph 3 = suggestion 2 – tell the girl, why this is a good idea
Paragraph 4 = Conclusion – more reassurance, and general advice

2 First, you could decide to say nothing./Second, you could tell the girl how you feel.

3 Yes

6 (*Students' own answers*)

Time to revise 2

Grammar

1 **1** 'll be lying **2** get/have got, 'll ring
3 'm seeing **4** will have made
5 's going to be **6** 'm going
7 does your flight leave? **8** were going
9 leave/have left **10** won't forget

2 **1** didn't have to go
2 could have asked for
3 should be doing/ought to be doing
4 ought not to have used
5 doesn't need to work/needn't work

3 **1** B **2** D **3** B **4** A **5** A **6** C

4 **1** are/get **2** to
3 will **4** must
5 a **6** can
7 what **8** have
9 be **10** enough
11 or **12** time

Vocabulary

5 **1** creative **2** fitness
3 hopeless **4** specialise
5 fizzy **6** priceless
7 completely **8** instructions

6 **1** retire **2** get on
3 job **4** as
5 make **6** employee
7 arrogant **8** makes
9 experience **10** losing

7 **1** B **2** A **3** B **4** C **5** D **6** B **7** C **8** B

Unit 5

Vocabulary 1

1 **1** f **2** h **3** c **4** g **5** d **6** a **7** e **8** b

2 **1** learn **2** write
3 break **4** play

3 **1** in **2** on
3 on **4** in
5 in

4 **1** muck about **2** rely
3 predicts **4** involves

Reading

1 **1** D **2** C **3** B **4** A **5** C **6** B **7** C **8** D

Vocabulary 2

1 **1** detention **2** expelled
3 dormitory **4** gown
5 strict **6** experiment
7 timetable **8** staff

2 **1** pass **2** achieve
3 fail **4** miss
5 professor **6** teacher
7 control **8** punish
9 grades **10** notes

3 **1** make **2** did
3 take **4** doing
5 make **6** take
7 made **8** done

4 **1** hand in **2** catch up
3 put off **4** work out
5 get through **6** falling behind

5 **1** A **2** B **3** B **4** A **5** B

Grammar

1

Adjective/ adverb	Comparative	Superlative
hot	hotter	the hottest
easy	easier	the easiest
hard	harder	the hardest
carefully	more carefully	the most carefully
good	better	the best
bad	worse	the worst
far	farther/further	the farthest/furthest
comfortable	more comfortable	the most comfortable
little	less	the least
many	more	the most

2 1 less interesting than
2 such an easy exam (that)
3 fast/quick enough to catch
4 the most thrilling novel I
5 so bored in the lesson (that) I
6 you work, the better grades
7 is too dangerous for children
8 such bad weather (that) we
9 wasn't as bad as/was better than
10 basketball better than

3 1 little   **2** a few
3 few   **4** a little

4 1 None of   **2** much
3 plenty   **4** much
5 too few

5 1 few   **2** all
3 few   **4** lot
5 plenty/lots   **6** little
7 few   **8** no
9 a

Use your English

1 1 great   **2** few
3 great/large   **4** lot
5 too   **6** more
7 less   **8** as
9 enough   **10** little
11 such   **12** the
13 than   **14** better
15 so

2 1 C **2** C **3** A **4** A **5** B **6** D **7** D **8** B
9 A **10** C **11** D **12** D **13** B **14** B

Writing *an essay*

1 1 your teacher
2 neutral/formal
3 - to mention both sides of the argument
4 (*Open answer*)
5 (*Open answer*)

2

Reasons to agree	Reasons against
2 It's a great place to make friends and see them all the time.	**1** You have to do what you're told.
3 Learning new things can be exciting.	**4** You may be stuck all day in class with people you don't like.
6 You don't need to worry about things like money.	**5** It's hard to sit and listen all day.
8 You've got very few responsibilities.	**7** It's boring having to study subjects you don't like.

3 It's rubbish to say that …

4 However, …

5 Paragraph 1 Introduction
Paragraph 2 my opinion
Paragraph 3 reservations/why some people might disagree with my opinion
Paragraph 4 Conclusion

6 1

7 (*Students' own answers*)

Unit 6

Vocabulary 1

1 1 careful   **2** curvy
3 glamorous   **4** healthy
5 hunky   **6** muscular
7 skinny   **8** trendy

2 1 trendy   **2** health
3 skinny   **4** glamorous
5 care   **6** muscular

3 1 eyebrow   **2** freckle(s)
3 double chin   **4** stubble
5 wrinkle   **6** spots
7 fringe

4 1 worry   **2** resist
3 wasted   **4** matter
5 kidding   **6** risked
7 blames/blamed   **8** ruined

Reading

1 1 H **2** C **3** A **4** D **5** G **6** B **7** E
Sentence F is not needed

Vocabulary 2

1 1 c **2** j **3** g **4** b **5** d **6** f **7** h **8** a
9 e **10** i

2 1 short black leather
2 fabulous long baggy
3 funky green canvas
4 beautiful long Chinese silk
5 dirty old rubber

3 1 tongue   **2** leg
3 head   **4** neck
5 eye   **6** hand

4 1 fit   **2** wear
3 looks   **4** match
5 dress

Grammar

1 1 A 2 B 3 B 4 B 5 B

2 1 'll be, leave 2 would get, had
3 lost 4 will wear, promise
5 always shrink, wash 6 see, will ask

3 1 had worn 2 were
3 hadn't lost 4 have done
5 don't 6 had had

4 1 says
2 have, sometimes hurts
3 wouldn't put, were
4 pays
5 had known, would have worn
6 finish/have finished

5 1 e 2 g 3 f 4 h 5 a 6 c 7 d 8 b

Use your English

1 1 I were you, I would 2 if she had spoken
3 unless they eat 4 it hadn't rained
5 would be able to 6 unless you help
7 you were free 8 would still be working

2 1 D 2 C 3 B 4 C 5 B 6 D 7 A 8 D
9 D 10 B 11 A 12 C 13 A

Writing *a formal letter*

1 1 Mike Storm/The producer of a TV company
2 a neutral/formal style

2 (*Open answers*)

3 2 Dear Mr Storm,
4 I am writing to give you my ideas on your next TV series for teens.
6 I hope my ideas are helpful.
8 Yours sincerely,

4 2 Your last programme was just awful. (I'm afraid I wasn't very keen on your last programme.)
4 I insist that you include hair-styling in your list of topics. (I think it would be a good idea to include hair-styling in your list of topics./I suggest you include hair-styling in your list of topics.)

5 1 First, … ✓
2 What's more, … ✓
3 Furthermore, … ✓
4 Turning to your question about … ✗
5 Secondly, … ✓
6 Finally, … ✓
7 As regards … ✗

6 (*Suggested answer*)
Paragraph 1 Introduction. Say why I'm writing (to give my comments on the new TV show).
Paragraph 2 say why I think it's a good idea to aim the series at teens. Say which days would be best and why.
Paragraph 3 suggest they include items like fashion, body-decoration, designer stuff, diet and health
Paragraph 4 explain why I didn't like the series on fashion models
Paragraph 5 Final comments + closing phrase

7 (*Students' own answers*)

Time to revise 3

Grammar

1 1 least 2 the
3 most/least 4 so
5 as 6 better/nicer
7 too 8 enough
9 worst 10 in

2 1 had known, would have gone
2 loses, won't be able
3 could, had
4 wouldn't join, were
5 need, give
6 had told
7 will come, don't get
8 won
9 stay, always worry
10 would/could have slept, hadn't woken

3 1 A 2 D 3 A 4 C 5 B 6 C

4 1 too hot to study
2 as expensive as
3 in case you see somebody
4 the biggest we have (ever)
5 not old enough to get
6 were you I would
7 too quickly for me to
8 had not been texting

Vocabulary

5 1 unknown 2 disappearance
3 designer 4 unattractive
5 shabbily 6 straightened
7 beautiful 8 glamorous

6 1 spots 2 have
3 match 4 made
5 like 6 grades
7 dresses 8 heart

7 1 C 2 B 3 A 4 D 5 D 6 B 7 C 8 A

Unit 7

Vocabulary 1

1   **1** B   **2** A   **3** A   **4** B   **5** B   **6** A   **7** A   **8** B

2
1	improve	**2**	solve
3	admit	**4**	measure
5	composed	**6**	view
7	purchase	**8**	competed

3
1	visitors	**2**	performance
3	admission	**4**	activities
5	scientists	**6**	researcher

Reading

1   **1** C   **2** D   **3** B   **4** A   **5** C   **6** D   **7** B   **8** C
    9 A   **10** D

Vocabulary 2

1
1	screen	**2**	mouse
3	virtual	**4**	keyboard
5	chat room	**6**	website
7	online	**8**	download

2
1	scientist	**2**	mathematician
3	astronomer	**4**	chemist
5	geologist	**6**	engineer
7	physicist	**8**	biologist

3   **1** B   **2** A   **3** B   **4** B   **5** A   **6** B   **7** B   **8** A

4
1	high-tech	**2**	network
3	interactive	**4**	webpage
5	software	**6**	hard drive

Grammar

1
1. is closed
2. has just been sent
3. was completed
4. Will the machine be repaired /Will the machine have been repaired
5. was being interviewed
6. had been stolen

2
1. Passive
2. ✓ Visitors are being shown round the new exhibit.
3. Passive
4. ✓ The test was being carried out by nuclear scientists.
5. ✓ The chemicals can't have been stolen.
6. Passive
7. ✓ The experiment must be done with care.
8. ✓ We were made to clear up the broken test tubes.
9. ✓ We were allowed to try out the new computers.
10. Passive

3   **1** A   **2** B   **3** B   **4** B

4
1. our computer fixed
2. it serviced
3. his eyes tested
4. his mobile phone stolen
5. the car tyres checked
6. your name been

5
1. He had his wallet stolen while he was shopping.
2. We managed to get the work done in time.
3. Why don't you have your initials engraved on your mobile phone?
4. She ought to get her hair cut.
5. Why haven't you had your watch repaired?
6. Did you get your photo taken last night?

Use your English

1
1. have
2. are
3. been
4. has
5. is
6. was/is
7. made/forced/asked/told/ordered
8. it
9. by
10. be
11. may/could/might
12. have/get
13. will

2   **1** A   **2** B   **3** C   **4** D   **5** C   **6** D   **7** B   **8** A
    9 D   **10** C   **11** D   **12** A   **13** B

Writing *a review*

1
1. A teen magazine. Teenagers (ages 13-19)
2. semi-formal/informal
3. an adventure/action or a spy movie
4. the stunts, the plot

2 Review should be paragraphed as follows (there could be one more paragraph starting with sentence 'The stunts are excellent' and finishing with … 'driven at high speed.').

Casino Royale is a spy film and is part of the James Bond series. It stars Daniel Craig as the first blond Bond.
The plot is brilliant. Bond is sent to Madagascar, where he finds out about a group of terrorists. He is ordered to defeat their banker in a game of cards at a casino. He falls in love with his assistant and promises to leave the secret service for her. But she betrays him.
There are fewer gadgets than in previous Bond movies, and this makes the whole thing more realistic. Bond's incredible Aston Martin is featured, of course, and Bond carries his usual gun. The stunts are excellent.

In one scene, a police car is thrown high into the air by a moving aeroplane. In another, Bond's Aston Martin is made to roll over seven times while being driven at high speed.
This is a tough, violent movie and is definitely not suitable for kids under twelve. But if you're over thirteen and you're looking for a movie full of action and suspense, you'll love it!

3 Casino Royale is a spy film and is part of the James Bond series. It stars Daniel Craig as the first blond Bond. The plot is <u>brilliant</u>. Bond is sent to Madagascar, where he finds out about a group of terrorists. He is ordered to defeat their banker in a game of cards at a casino. He falls in love with his assistant and promises to leave the secret service for her. But she betrays him. There are fewer gadgets than in previous Bond movies, and this makes the whole thing more realistic. Bond's incredible Aston Martin is featured, of course, and Bond carries his usual gun. The stunts are <u>excellent</u>. <u>In one scene</u>, a police car is thrown high into the air by a moving aeroplane. <u>In another</u>, Bond's Aston Martin is made to roll over seven times while being driven at high speed. <u>This is a tough, violent movie and is definitely not suitable for kids under twelve. But if you're over thirteen and you're looking for a movie full of action and suspense, you'll love it!</u>

4 There should be a minimum of four paragraphs, and not more than five. Suggested answer:
Paragraph 1 (Introduction) name and type of film, main actors/characters
Paragraph 2 short summary of the plot/what happens in the film. (present tenses)
Paragraph 3 short description of stunts/gadgets (present tenses, maybe some passives)
Paragraph 4 (Conclusion) whether the movie is suitable for teens and why

6 (*Students' own answers*)

Unit 8

Vocabulary 1

1
1	to	**2**	on
3	into	**4**	in
5	at	**6**	off
7	of	**8**	to
9	from	**10**	by

2
1	persuaded	**2**	concentrate
3	decreased	**4**	promote
5	accused	**6**	survived
7	runs	**8**	battle
9	improved	**10**	campaigning

Reading

1 **1** C **2** C **3** B **4** A **5** E **6** B **7** A, D
8 F **9** C **10** F **11** C **12** E **13** B **14** D

Vocabulary 2

1
1	chef	**2**	fizzy
3	nutritious	**4**	recipe
5	delicious	**6**	ingredients
7	junk	**8**	diet

2 **1** B **2** A **3** B **4** B **5** A

3
1	cabbage	**2**	pineapple
3	cheese	**4**	lamb
5	salmon	**6**	peach

4
1	give	**2**	wash
3	do	**4**	go
5	put	**6**	run
7	cut	**8**	make

5
1	on	**2**	out
3	in	**4**	on
5	out	**6**	in
7	out	**8**	at

Grammar

1
1	to understand	**2**	doing
3	Playing	**4**	eating
5	coming	**6**	eating
7	stay	**8**	getting
9	to see	**10**	let

2
1	to come	**2**	getting up
3	preparing	**4**	training
5	to wash up	**6**	try
7	take part	**8**	to eating
9	help	**10**	to walk

3
1	to have	**2**	having
3	buying	**4**	to buy
5	eating	**6**	to eat
7	to tell	**8**	telling
9	to be	**10**	being

4 **1** A **2** A **3** B **4** A **5** A **6** B

Use your English

1 **1** C **2** D **3** B **4** A **5** B **6** B **7** D **8** C
9 A **10** C

2 **1** C **2** D **3** B **4** D **5** A **6** D **7** D **8** B
9 C **10** C

3 **1** impossible to play
2 advise you to go swimming
3 accused me of breaking
4 let me light
5 suggest we go/going
6 gave up smoking

Writing *a report*

1 **1** your head teacher   **2** a neutral style

2 – your opinion about whether pupils should pay to join the Club
– your opinion about whether your school needs a Club or not

3 **Activities to offer**
suggestions about/descriptions of what people could do in the Club
Place and time
suggestions about when and where the Club should meet
Recruiting members
suggestions about ways to advertise the Club

4 **2** **To:** The head teacher
Subject: The Health and Fitness Club
Introduction: The purpose of this report is to make suggestions for our new Club.

5 **2** **Conclusion**
I hope the suggestions in this report will help to make our Club successful.

6 **1** I suggest the Club meets/should meet at least twice a week because it is important to exercise regularly to get fit.
2 I recommend we put/putting posters on our school noticeboards so everyone can read/will read about the Club.
3 I think we should offer a range of activities, both indoor and outdoor, so we are/can be sure there is something for everyone.

7 (*Students' own answers*)

Time to revise 4

Grammar

1 **1** in   **2** been
3 may   **4** has
5 by   **6** was
7 up   **8** like
9 are   **10** is
11 being   **12** a/any

2 **1** You must get that jacket cleaned soon.
2 She just managed to get her homework finished on time.
3 Why don't you get your hair dyed like mine?
4 He has got to have his watch repaired.
5 I am thinking of getting a heart tattooed on my arm!
6 She had her purse stolen in the market yesterday.
7 I've got to have these jeans taken up.
8 When did he last have his eyes tested?

3 **1** C **2** B **3** A **4** D **5** A **6** B **7** D **8** C

Vocabulary

4 **1** inventions   **2** gadget
3 experiment   **4** researching
5 bill   **6** download
7 plug   **8** junk
9 surfing   **10** laugh

5 **1** C **2** B **3** A **4** C **5** D **6** B

6 **1** B **2** C **3** A **4** D **5** A **6** C **7** D **8** A
9 B **10** C **11** D **12** A

Unit 9

Vocabulary 1

1 **1** label   **2** victim
3 appeal   **4** accessories
5 logo   **6** symbol
7 lifestyle   **8** product

2 **1** In   **2** at
3 out   **4** in
5 on   **6** for

3 **1** original   **2** fashionable
3 fortunately   **4** knowledge
5 designer   **6** trainers
7 advertising

Reading

1 **1** G **2** E **3** F **4** D **5** H **6** B **7** A
Sentence C is not needed

Vocabulary 2

1 **1** victim   **2** store
3 symbol   **4** name
5 label   **6** market

2 **1** off   **2** up
3 out of   **4** among
5 out

3 **1** exclusive   **2** flattering
3 trendy   **4** stereotyped
5 sophisticated

4 1 persuasive   2 advertisement
3 luxurious   4 appealing
5 competition   6 promotion

5 1 d   2 e   3 a   4 c   5 b

6 1 B   2 A   3 B   4 B   5 A   6 B   7 A   8 B

Grammar

1 1 me to go   2 had stolen
3 told   4 whether the sale had begun
5 had closed   6 not to spend

2 1 told Tom/him (that) is was
2 know when the shop (would)
3 asked if I could try
4 to close the bag
5 said (that) they had spent their
6 told/ordered me not to touch
7 realised (that) she had forgotten
8 inquired if/whether I needed

3 1 A   2 B   3 B   4 A   5 A   6 B   7 A   8 B

4 1 breaking   2 not to touch
3 to buy   4 stealing
5 to blow up

5 1 to go   2 taking
3 to check   4 to try on
5 wasting   6 having
7 to show   8 to leave
9 having to   10 not to worry

Use your English

1 1 B   2 C   3 A   4 D   5 C   6 B   7 A   8 D
9 C   10 B   11 A   12 C   13 D

2 1 on   2 if
3 to   4 would
5 going   6 we
7 on   8 tried/put
9 told   10 her
11 of   12 for
13 the

Writing *an email*

1 1 your penfriend   2 an informal, chatty style

2 (*Open answers*)

3 (*Open answers*)

4

Asking about preferences/ Making suggestions	Referring to a new topic
Would you like to …	You asked about …
Do you fancy …ing?	Regarding your suggestion about …
We could …	Turning to your question about …
I suggest that we …	Now, about …

5 **Paragraph 1** (Introduction) opening remarks
Paragraph 2 ask George what he'd prefer to do for his birthday
Paragraph 3 say whether there are markets near here and give details
Paragraph 4 say what Mum and Dad would like as a present, and why
Paragraph 5 say whether it's a good idea to meet George's friend and make a suggestion
Paragraph 6 (Conclusion) Closing remarks

6 (*Students' own answers*)

Unit 10

Vocabulary 1

1 1 harmless   2 rebellious
3 exciting   4 vandalise
5 guilty   6 imprison
7 reality   8 punishment
9 eventually   10 signature

2 1 at   2 in
3 on   4 along
5 in   6 in
7 at   8 at
9 in   10 out

3 1 break   2 learn
3 get   4 change
5 pass   6 go
7 play   8 rob

Reading

1 1 A   2 D   3 B   4 C   5 A   6 B   7 D   8 C
9 A   10 D   11 B   12 A   13 D   14 C   15 B
16 D

Vocabulary 2

1 1 innocent   2 court
3 murdered   4 witness
5 sentenced   6 attacked

2 1 d   2 f   3 a   4 e   5 c   6 b

3 **1** with   **2** on
3 for   **4** from
5 of   **6** for

4 **1** lawyer   **2** jury
3 gang   **4** conviction
5 evidence   **6** ringleader
7 case   **8** court

5

Crime	Verb	Person
1 shoplifting	*to shoplift*	*a shoplifter*
2 *forgery*	to forge	*a forger*
3 mugging	*to mug*	a mugger
4 *burglary*	to burgle	*a burglar*
5 *robbery*	*to rob*	a robber
6 theft	to thieve/to steal	*a thief*
7 *murder*	to murder	*a murderer*
8 *fraud*	to defraud	a fraudster
9 vandalism	*to vandalise*	a vandal
10 assault	*to assault*	an assailant

6 **1** B   **2** A   **3** B   **4** A   **5** B

7 **1** shoplifting   **2** mugged
3 forged   **4** vandalising
5 murdered   **6** tricked

Grammar

1 **1** wouldn't   **2** hadn't joined
3 breaking   **4** shouldn't have written
5 were   **6** could

2 **1** knew   **2** hadn't stolen
3 would leave   **4** telling
5 had

3 **1** B   **2** A   **3** B   **4** A   **5** B   **6** A

4 **1** could   **2** order
3 so   **4** and
5 to   **6** as
7 of   **8** were
9 had   **10** have
11 the   **12** as
13 such

Use your English

1 **1** amazing   **2** Criminals
3 variety   **4** information
5 copied   **6** advice
7 valuable   **8** careful
9 extremely   **10** knowledge
11 worried

2 **1** not telling
2 in case the alarm rang
3 in order to catch
4 shouldn't have stolen
5 such a valuable painting that
6 he was very strong
7 wished he were a police officer
8 only I had reported

Writing *an essay*

1 **2** ✓

2 (*Open answers*)

3 (*Open answers*)

4 **1** g   **2** a   **3** f   **4** h   **5** e   **6** b   **7** d   **8** c

5 **1** On the other hand   **2** What's more
3 in order to   **4** In fact
5 As a result

6 **Paragraph 1** introductory statements
Paragraph 2 reasons why I think children with working mothers are/are not likely to get involved in crime
Paragraph 3 what people with an opposite view to me think, and why. Why I still think my views outweigh theirs.
Paragraph 4 A summary/restatement of my opinions

7 **8** (*Students' own answers*)

Time to revise 5

Grammar

1 **1** case   **2** on
3 a   **4** While
5 denied   **6** could
7 breaking   **8** told

2 **1** whether he could have
2 wishes she hadn't bought
3 suggested having/that we had
4 apologised for breaking
5 accused me of stealing
6 should not/shouldn't have told
7 I could afford
8 warned me not to leave

3 **1** B   **2** B   **3** D   **4** A   **5** B   **6** C

Vocabulary

4 **1** store   **2** market
3 card   **4** room
5 detective   **6** shopping
7 symbol   **8** have

5 **1** misunderstood **2** trial
3 defraud **4** dishonest
5 disobey **6** infamous
7 disrespect **8** punishment

6 **1** arrested **2** appeal
3 off **4** out of
5 accessories **6** witness
7 commit **8** stricter

7 **1** B **2** D **3** A **4** C **5** D **6** B

Unit 11

Vocabulary 1

1 **1** gasped **2** peered
3 inscribed **4** threatened
5 wondered **6** survived
7 spread **8** disturbs
9 gathered **10** ignoring

2 **1** at **2** in
3 In **4** with
5 in

3 **1** wound **2** spirit/soul
3 reign **4** enemies
5 charm **6** exhausted

Reading

1 **1** B **2** A **3** B **4** C **5** C **6** C **7** D **8** C

Vocabulary 2

1 **1** threatened **2** burial
3 homeless **4** punishment
5 excavation **6** lucky
7 death **8** strengthened
9 length **10** archaeological

2 **1** rumour **2** chariots
3 history **4** facts
5 shrine

3 **1** A **2** A **3** B **4** A **5** B **6** B **7** B

4 **1** scanned **2** gazing
3 glimpsed **4** glared
5 peered

Grammar

1 **1** can't be
2 must be imagining
3 Could it have escaped
4 may be
5 must be going

2 **1** are believed, have built
2 is said, lived in trees
3 are claimed to, killing
4 is thought to be

3 **1** couldn't have seen
2 said to be living
3 must have been digging
4 is believed that
5 could/might be
6 are thought to be
7 may have been murdered by
8 can't have been listening

Use your English

1 **1** A **2** be
3 is **4** which
5 to **6** could/might
7 are **8** ago
9 have **10** be
11 was **12** so
13 its

2 **1** D **2** C **3** B **4** D **5** A **6** C **7** B **8** D
9 C **10** A **11** C **12** A

Writing *a story*

1 (*Open answers*)

2 Answers should follow this main pattern:
Paragraph 1 (Introduction) Set the scene.
Paragraph 2 ...first events
Paragraph 3 ...what happened next
Paragraph 4 (Conclusion + prompt sentence from writing task) end of story

3 Sarah woke up with a jump and opened her eyes. Everyone in the tent was sleeping. They had been travelling all day. No wonder they were **tired**!
Sarah stepped outside. She and her friends had chosen to camp near the forest because it was so **quiet**. But in the dark, it looked unwelcoming and **frightening**. She was getting back into the tent when she suddenly heard a **strange** noise. Something was moving about at the edge of the trees. The forest was said to be haunted. Feeling **scared**, Sarah peered into the darkness.

4 Sarah woke up with a jump and opened her eyes. Everyone in the tent was sleeping. They had been travelling all day. No wonder they were **exhausted**!

Sarah stepped outside. She and her friends had chosen to camp near the forest because it was so **peaceful**. But in the dark, it looked unwelcoming and **spooky**. She was getting back into the tent when she suddenly heard a **bizarre** noise. Something was moving about at the edge of the trees. The forest was said to be haunted. Feeling **terrified**, Sarah peered into the darkness.

5 At first, she couldn't make out anything. But as her eyes grew accustomed to the darkness, she saw a huge shape. 'Is it animal or human?' she wondered. She stood and watched as the thing came nearer. It was huge and very hairy!

6 2

7 (*Students' own answers*)

Unit 12

Vocabulary 1

1 1 national 2 white-knuckle 3 adventure 4 camping 5 native 6 white-water 7 coach 8 roller

2 1 scenery 2 cliff(s) 3 destination 4 exhilarating/exciting 5 wilderness 6 awesome/amazing

3 1 activities 2 incredible 3 instructor 4 luxurious 5 magical 6 wildlife

Reading

1 1 D 2 B 3 C 4 C 5 D 6 A 7 D 8 C

Vocabulary 2

1 1 b 2 d 3 a 4 i 5 e 6 g 7 c 8 f 9 h 10 j

2 1 jam 2 pass/card 3 office 4 lounge 5 rack 6 pack

3 1 B 2 A 3 A 4 A 5 B 6 A

4 1 a journey b tour c travel 2 a way b road c path 3 a view b scenery c scene

5 1 for 2 in 3 on 4 on 5 of 6 for 7 in 8 of 9 about 10 on

Grammar

1 1 B 2 D 3 C 4 A 5 C 6 D

2 1 The castle, which we visited on day two of our holiday, was destroyed in the 15th century.
2 They've managed to book the holiday they wanted to go on.
3 Can you see the bird I'm looking at?
4 They camped out in the rainforest, which was the best part of their holiday.
5 Have you seen the guide who is/who's supposed to take us round?
6 I'm staying with a friend whose relatives own a yacht.
7 We went to a theme park, which was a brilliant experience.
8 Yellowstone, which is a national park, is home to a great number of bears.

3 1 eating lunch, we went to the beach.
2 we'd missed our flight, we went home.
3 never been on a roller coaster, she was a bit nervous.
4 a wild bear near our tents, we ran away.
5 first in the queue, we got a good seat on the coach.
6 winning/having won the competition, he bought himself a surfboard.

Use your English

1 1 in 2 more 3 It 4 when 5 known 6 who 7 where 8 to 9 which 10 of 11 plenty/lots 12 most 13 with

2 1 D 2 A 3 B 4 C 5 B 6 A 7 D 8 A 9 A 10 C 11 A 12 B 13 C

Writing *an article*

1 1 readers of a teen magazine
2 lively and chatty
3 a description of the holiday; reasons why it would appeal to teenagers

2 (*Open answers*)

3 2

4 <u>Kruger Park is in the north-east of South Africa.</u> To get there, you have to fly to Johannesburg, then change flights. It's a long journey but very worthwhile!

<u>The Park is awesome.</u> It covers a huge area, and a lot of it is parched dry in summer. It's home to lions, elephants, rhinos and lots more wildlife, which you can see when you go on safari. The best way to get about is on the back of an elephant! You feel really safe up there, and none of the animals you want to see are scared of you. You can feed your elephant too, and swim with it - it's really good fun!

5 1

6 2

7 Suggested paragraph plan:
Paragraph 1 (Introduction) name of the place and fact that it's good for teens
Paragraph 2 where it is, how to get there
Paragraph 3 what it's like, what you can do there
Paragraph 4 (Conclusion) any other aspects of the holiday, a recommendation

8 (*Students' own answers*)

Time to revise 6

Grammar

1
1	must	**2**	lost
3	have gone	**4**	to be
5	which	**6**	whose
7	which	**8**	getting

2
1	have	**2**	the
3	be	**4**	where
5	more	**6**	in
7	who	**8**	which
9	in	**10**	whose
11	one	**12**	to

3
1 can't have landed
2 is believed that
3 I've/I have ever eaten in
4 must have been flying
5 having failed her exams,
6 said to be growing
7 whose this jacket is/whose jacket this is
8 I spoke to was

Vocabulary

4
1	campsite	**2**	sleeping bag
3	check-in desk	**4**	traffic jam
5	backpack	**6**	one-way street
7	skydiving	**8**	boarding pass/card

5
1	behaviour	**2**	breadth
3	burial	**4**	belief
5	settlement	**6**	strength
7	death	**8**	undisturbed

6
1	fiction	**2**	tomb
3	chariots	**4**	rumour
5	hoax	**6**	journey
7	situated	**8**	go

7
1	in	**2**	for
3	of	**4**	round
5	on	**6**	on/of
7	over/around	**8**	on